The Assassination of Benazir Bhutto

The Assassination of Benazir Bhutto

Yasir Hussain

Epitome Books
New Delhi

First edition 2008

Published by
Epitome Books
B-65 Mansaram Park
Near Nawada Metro Station
New Delhi – 110 059

Cataloging in Publication Data–DK
Courtesy: D.K. Agencies (P) Ltd. <docinfo@dkagencies.com>

Hussain, Yasir, 1976-
The assassination of Benazir Bhutto / Yasir Hussain.
p. cm.
Benazir Bhutto, 1953-2007, former Prime Minister of Pakistan.
Includes bibliographical references (p.)
Includes index.

ISBN 13: 978-81-906260-4-0 ISBN 10: 81-906260-4-3

1. Bhutto, Benazir, 1953-2007--Assassination. 2. Prime ministers--Assassination--Pakistan. 3. Pakistan--Politics and government--1988- I. Title.

DDC 954.910 509 2 22

Printed at Salasar Imaging Systems, Delhi - 35

PREFACE

Benazir Bhutto (born 1953) became the first woman head of government in the Muslim world when she was elected prime minister of Pakistan in 1988, only to be deposed in a coup 20 months later. She was re-elected in 1993 but was dismissed three years later amid various corruption scandals. Some of these scandals involve contracts awarded to Swiss companies during her regime and remain unresolved. Her husband has been implicated as well.

The daughter of former Pakistani premier, Zulfikar Ali Bhutto, Benazir Bhutto was educated in the west, notably at Harvard University, and Lady Margaret Hall, Oxford. She temporarily left Harvard for New York City in 1971, when India sent troops into East Pakistan soon to be called Bangladesh and her father, as West Pakistan's foreign minister, travelled to the United Nations to resolve the issue. Benazir Bhutto joined her father in New York City and acted as a kind of assistant to him. This seems to have been a formative experience for her, in that watching her father in action brought her out of the academy and showed her the ways of power politics. Her remaining years in the United States included active participation in various social causes.

During her time at Oxford, she was President of the Oxford Union, after the election had to be re-run because she accused her rival of illegal canvassing. Her entire undergraduate career was fuelled by controversy, coming in the middle of a period when her father's administration was being challenged both at home and abroad.

After graduating, she returned to Pakistan, but, in the course of her father's imprisonment and execution, she was placed under house arrest. Having been allowed, in 1984, to go back to the UK, she was leader in exile of her father's party, but was unable to make her political presence felt in Pakistan until the death of General Zia-ul-Haq.

Then in the first open election in more than a decade, voters in Pakistan chose populist candidate Benazir Bhutto on November 16, 1988 to be Prime Minister. Bhutto was sworn-in on December 2, 1988, becoming the first woman to head the government of an Islamic state

Bhutto has lived in self-imposed exile since 1999 when she left Pakistan to avoid arrest in a corruption case. She still heads the Pakistan People's Party and says she wants to return to office. Her husband, Asif Ali Zardari, has also served a seven-year prison term in Pakistan on charges of taking kickbacks.

It was during Bhutto's rule that the repressive Taliban gained prominence in Afghanistan with the financial assistance of her government. The Taliban took power in Kabul in September 1996, and Pakistan was a key supporter of the regime until the September 11 attacks in the United States.

In 2002, Pakistan's current military President, Pervez Musharaf introduced a new amendment to Pakistan's constitution, banning Prime Ministers from serving more than two terms.

Benazir Bhutto, the Pakistani opposition leader and twice-serving prime minister, was assassinated on Dec 27, 2007 as she left a political rally here, a scene of fiery carnage that plunged Pakistan deeper into political turmoil and ignited widespread violence by her enraged supporters. Ms. Bhutto, 54, was shot in the neck or head, according to differing accounts, as she stood in the open sunroof of a car and waved to crowds. Seconds later a suicide attacker detonated his bomb, damaging one of the cars in her motorcade, killing more than 20 people and wounding 50.

CONTENTS

1

Benazir Bhutto Great Leader of Pakistan

Mohtarma Benazir Bhutto (June 21, 1953 – December 27, 2007) was a Pakistani politician who chaired the Pakistan People's Party (PPP), a centre-left political party in Pakistan. Bhutto was the first woman elected to lead a Muslim state, having twice been Prime Minister of Pakistan (1988–1990 and 1993–1996).

Bhutto was the eldest child of former prime minister Zulfikar Ali Bhutto, a Pakistani of Sindhi descent and Shia Muslim by faith, and Begum Nusrat Bhutto, a Pakistani of Iranian-Kurdish descent, of similarly Shia Muslim by faith. Her paternal grandfather was Sir Shah Nawaz Bhutto, who came to Larkana Sindh before partition from his native town of Bhatto Kalan, which was situated in the Indian state of Haryana.

Bhutto was sworn in as the Prime Minister of Pakistan for the first time in 1988 at the age of 35, but was removed from office 20 months later under the order of then-president Ghulam Ishaq Khan on grounds of alleged corruption. In 1993, Bhutto was re-elected but was again removed in 1996 on similar charges, this time by President Farooq Leghari. Bhutto went into self-imposed exile in Dubai in 1998.

Bhutto returned to Pakistan on October 18, 2007, after reaching an understanding with President Pervez Musharraf by which she was granted amnesty and all corruption charges were withdrawn. She was assassinated on December 27, 2007, when she was returning from a PPP rally in Rawalpindi, two weeks before the scheduled general elections on January 8, 2008 where she was a leading opposition candidate.

Education and Life

Benazir Bhutto was born to Begum Nusrat Bhutto, and Zulfikar Ali Bhutto on June 21, 1953. She attended the Lady Jennings Nursery School and then the Convent of Jesus and Mary in Karachi. After two years of schooling at the Rawalpindi Presentation Convent, she was sent to the Jesus and Mary Convent at Murree. She passed her O-level examinations at the age of 15. She then went on to complete her A-Levels at the Karachi Grammar School.

After completing her early education in Pakistan, she pursued her higher education in the United States. From 1969 to 1973, she attended Radcliffe College at Harvard University, where she obtained a Bachelor of Arts degree with *cum laude* honors in comparative government. She was also elected to Phi Beta Kappa. Bhutto would later call her time at Harvard "four of the happiest years of my life" and said it formed "the very basis of [her] belief in democracy".

The next phase of her education took place in the United Kingdom. Between 1973 and 1977, Bhutto studied Philosophy, Politics, and Economics at Lady Margaret Hall, Oxford, during which time she completed additional courses in International Law and Diplomacy. In December 1976, she was elected president of the Oxford Union, becoming the first Asian woman to head the prestigious society.

On December 18, 1987, she married Asif Ali Zardari in Karachi. The couple had three children: Bilawal, Bakhtwar and Aseefa.

Family

Benazir Bhutto's father, former Prime Minister Zulfikar Ali Bhutto, was removed from office following a military coup in 1977 led by the then military chief General Muhammad Zia-ul-Haq, who imposed martial law but promised to hold elections within three months. But later, instead of fulfilling the promise of holding general elections, General Zia charged Mr. Bhutto with conspiring to murder the father of dissident politician Ahmed Raza Kasuri. Mr. Zulfikar Ali Bhutto was sentenced to death by the martial law court.

Despite the accusation being "widely doubted by the public", and despite many clemency appeals from foreign leaders, Zulfikar Ali Bhutto was hanged on April 4, 1979. Appeals for clemency were dismissed by acting President General Zia. Benazir Bhutto and her mother were held in a "police camp" until the end of May, after the execution.

In 1985, Benazir Bhutto's brother Shahnawaz was killed under suspicious circumstances in France. The killing of of her second brother, Mir Murtaza, in 1996, contributed to destabilizing her second term as Prime Minister.

Prime Minister

Bhutto, who had returned to Pakistan after completing her studies, found herself placed under house arrest in the wake of her father's imprisonment and subsequent execution. Having been allowed in 1984 to return to the United Kingdom, she became a leader in exile of the PPP, her father's party, though she was unable to make her political presence felt in Pakistan until after the death of General Muhammad Zia-ul-Haq. She succeeded her mother as leader of the PPP and the pro-democracy campaign against the Zia-ul-Haq regime.

On November 16, 1988, in the first general elections in more than a decade, Bhutto's PPP won the largest seats in the National Assembly. Bhutto was sworn in as Prime Minister of a coalition government on December 2, becoming the youngest and first woman head of a muslim country. In 1989, she was awarded the Prize For Freedom by the Liberal

International. Bhutto's initiatives for nationalist reform and modernization were characterized as Westernization by some conservatives. Bhutto's government was dismissed in 1990 following charges of corruption, for which she never was tried. Zia's protégé Nawaz Sharif subsequently came to power. Bhutto was re-elected in 1993 but was dismissed three years later amid various corruption scandals by then President, Farooq Leghari, who used the Eighth Amendment discretionary powers to dissolve the government. The Supreme Court affirmed President Leghari's dismissal in a 6-1 ruling.

After being dismissed by the then President of Pakistan on charges of corruption, her party lost the October elections. She served as leader of the opposition whilst Nawaz Sharif served as Prime Minister for the next three years.

During the election campaigns the Bhutto government voiced its concern for women's social and health issues, including the issue of discrimination against women. Bhutto announced plans to establish women's police stations, courts, and women's development banks. Despite these plans, Bhutto did not propose any legislation to improve welfare services for women. During her election campaigns, she promised to repeal controversial laws (such as Hudood and Zina ordinances) that curtail the rights of women in Pakistan, but the party did not fulfill these promises during her tenures as Prime Minister, due to immense pressure from the opposition.

After Bhutto's stints as Prime Minister, during General Musharraf's regime, her party did initiate legislation to repeal the Zina ordinance. These efforts were defeated by the right-wing religious parties that dominated the legislature at the time. Bhutto was an active and founding member of the Council of Women World Leaders, a network of current and former prime ministers and presidents.

Arthur Herman, a U.S. historian, in a controversial letter published in *The Wall Street Journal* on June 14, 2007, in response to an article by Bhutto highly critical of the president and his policies, has described her as "One of the most incompetent leaders in the history of South Asia", and asserted that she and other elites in Pakistan hated Musharraf because he was a *muhajir*, the son of one of millions of Indian Muslims who fled to Pakistan during partition in 1947. Herman has claimed, "Although it was muhajirs who agitated for the creation of Pakistan in the first place, many native Pakistanis view them with contempt and treat them as third-class citizens."

Nonetheless, as of mid-2007, the US appeared to be pushing for a deal in which Musharraf would remain as President but step down as military head, and either Bhutto or one of her nominees would become prime minister.

On July 11, 2007, the Associated Press, in an article about the possible aftermath of the Red Mosque incident, wrote:

> *Benazir Bhutto, the former prime minister and opposition leader, expected by many to return from exile and join Musharraf in a power-sharing deal after year-end general elections, praised him for taking a tough line on the Red Mosque. I'm glad there was no ceasefire with the militants in the mosque because ceasefires simply embolden the militants," she told Britain's Sky TV. "There will be a backlash, but at some time we have to stop appeasing the militants."*

This remark about the Red Mosque was seen with dismay in Pakistan as reportedly hundreds of young students were burned to death and hundreds are untraceable and cases are being heard in Pakistani Supreme Court as a missing persons issue. This and subsequent support for Musharaf led Elder Bhutto's comrades like Khar to criticize her publicly.

Bhutto however advised Musharraf in an early phase of the latter's quarrel with the Chief Justice, to restore him. Her PPP did not capitalize on its CEC member, Aitzaz Ahsan, the chief Barrister for the Chief Justice, in successful restoration. Rather he was seen as a rival and was isolated.

Preparation for 2008 Elections

On November 24, 2007, Bhutto filed her nomination papers for January's Parliamentary elections. Two days later, she filed papers in the Larkana constituency for two regular seats. She did so as former Pakistani Prime Minister Nawaz

Sharif, following seven years of exile in Saudi Arabia, made his much-contested return to Pakistan and bid for candidacy.

When sworn in again on November 30, 2007, this time as a civilian president after relinquishing his post as military chief, Musharraf announced his plan to lift emergency on December 16. Bhutto welcomed the announcement and launched a manifesto outlining her party's domestic issues. Bhutto told journalists in Islamabad that her party, the PPP, would focus on "the five E's": employment, education, energy, environment, equality. On December 4, 2007, Bhutto met with Nawaz Sharif to publicize their demand that Musharraf fulfill his promise to lift the state of emergency before January's parliamentary elections, threatening to boycott the vote if he failed to comply. They promised to assemble a committee which would present to Musharraf the list of demands upon which their participation in the election was contingent.

On December 8, 2007, three unidentified gunmen stormed Bhutto's PPP office in the southern western province of Baluchistan. Three of Bhutto's supporters were killed.

Assassination

Benazir Bhutto had just addressed a rally of Pakistan People's Party (PPP) supporters in Rawalpindi when the rally was rocked by a blast. Bhutto was said to have been leaving the rally when the attack occurred. Initial police reports stated that one or more assassins fired at Bhutto's bulletproof white Toyota Land Cruiser just as she was about to drive off after the rally. A suicide bomber detonating a bomb next to her vehicle followed. According to Getty Images photographer John Moore, Bhutto was standing through her vehicle's sunroof to wave at supporters, and fell back inside after two gunshots, and the *Times of India* aired an amateur clip showing the assassin firing four gun shots at Bhutto before the blast. Her last words were "Long live Bhutto."

Following the incident, Bhutto was taken unconscious to the Rawalpindi General Hospital at 17:35 local time, where doctors led by Rawalpindi Medical College Principal

Mohammad Musaddiq Khan tried to resuscitate her, performing a "left anterolateral thoracotomy for open cardiac massage". Dr. Sadiq Khan, Khan's father, had tried to save Liaquat Ali Khan when he was assassinated in the same park and rushed to the same hospital in 1951. Although PPP spokesman Farhatullah Babar initially said that Bhutto was safe, she was declared dead at 18:16 local time (13:16 UTC).

Cause of Death

Initial reports based on Pakistani Interior Ministry information reported that Bhutto was killed by a gunshot wound to the neck. Rehman Malik, a security adviser for PPP, suggested that the killer opened fire as Bhutto left the rally and that he hit her in the neck and chest before he detonated the explosives he was wearing. Javed Cheema, an interior ministry spokesman, stated that her injuries were caused either by her having been shot or from pellets packed into the detonated bomb that acted as shrapnel.

On December 28, however, the cause of Bhutto's death became less clear. Pakistan's Interior Ministry announced that they now felt Bhutto's death was as a result of a neck fracture sustained when she ducked or fell into her vehicle and hit the sunroof catch immediately after the gunshots but later reported her cause of death as a skull fracture. According to an Associated Press report, the Ministry stated, "Bhutto was killed when she tried to duck back into the vehicle, and the shock waves from the blast knocked her head into a lever attached to the sunroof, fracturing her skull". The Ministry further added, in contradiction of the official hospital account, that Bhutto suffered no gunshot or shrapnel injuries and that all gunshots missed her.

PPP spokesman Farhatullah Babar rejected Bhutto's death having come as a result of an accident. Bhutto's lawyer and a senior official in PPP, Farooq Naik, said that the report was "baseless" and "a pack of lies." He went on to support the view that the cause of death was two bullets hitting Bhutto in the abdomen and the head. An anonymous

Toyota official also rejected the notion that she could have even hit the lever based on its location in the car (a Toyota Land Cruiser).

In statements made to Pakistan's *The News*, Mohammad Mussadiq Khan, one of the doctors who treated Bhutto at Rawalpindi General Hospital, described severe and depressed skull fractures, oval in overall shape, on the right side of Bhutto's head. He apparently saw no other injuries and downplayed the possibility of bullet wounds, although he had previously spoke of them. One anonymous doctor said that Pakistani authorities took Bhutto's medical records immediately after her death, and that they told doctors to stop talking.

On December 31, Athar Minallah of the Rawalpindi General Hospital released a statement (described as "clinical notes") signed by seven persons involved in Bhutto's treatment at the hospital. These persons were not pathologists and did not conduct a formal autopsy. The statement first narrates the course of treatment, from Bhutto's arrival at the hospital until she was declared dead. The second part of the statement details the head wound and notes that "Detailed external examination of the body did not reveal any other external injury". X-rays had been taken of the head wound and were interpreted in the statement. The cause of death was declared to be "Open head injury with depressed skull fracture, leading to cardiopulmonary arrest".

According to *The Washington Post*, the crime scene was cleared before any forensic examination could be completed and no formal autopsy was performed before burial. Doctors had asked permission to perform an autopsy, but this request was declined by the Rawalpindi chief of police. According to the BBC, Brigadier Cheema claims "They gave you absolute facts... collaborated by the doctors' report," and that Pakistan would allow her body to be exhumed.

On 1 January 2008, Pakistan's Interior Ministry backtracked on its statement that Benazir Bhutto had died from hitting her head on the sunroof latch. Ministry spokesman, Javed Iqbal Cheema said that the ministry would wait for forensic investigations before making a conclusion on Bhutto's cause of death.

Funeral

Bhutto's funeral occurred on the afternoon of 28 December 2007. Her body was moved from Chaklala Airbase in Rawalpindi to Sukkur Airport on December 28, 2007 at 1:20 a.m. Both her children and her husband travelled with her body. Earlier they reached Chaklala Air Base by a special flight to get her body. Mourners from all over Pakistan made their way to Larkana to take part in the funeral ceremony for the former Prime Minister. The family delivered the body to its site of burial via helicopter. Bhutto was laid to rest beside her father in the family tomb.

Aftermath

Riots

After Bhutto's death, supporters wept and broke the hospital's glass doors, threw stones at cars, and hundred abused on President Musharraf. Others attacked police and burned election campaign posters and tires. Some opposition groups said that the assassination could lead to civil war, and other commentators said that the upcoming elections would likely be postponed.

Demonstrations were widespread in Pakistan with police using tear gas and batons to break up angry demonstrations in Peshawar. Some protesters torched the billboards of Musharraf, firing in the air and screaming. Protests in Multan also had protesters burning tires and blocking traffic. Similar scenes were witnessed in Karachi, Bhutto's hometown. Police in Sindh have been put on red alert. The BBC broke the news that a police officer was shot in Karachi during the riots following the assassination.

Musharraf ordered a crack down on rioters and looters stating that they "must be dealt with firmly and all measures be taken to ensure [the] safety and security of the people". The Pakistan Rangers announced shoot-on-sight orders against anyone inciting violence or arson, although attempts to avoid direct confrontation were maintained. The next, the situation further deteriorated, especially in the Sindh Province, the homeground of Bhutto. Foreign outlets, trains, banks and vehicles were destroyed or burnt and protesters took over the streets, chanting slogans and setting tires on fire in several cities. At least 47 people died in the riots. Rioters destroyed 176 banks, 34 petrol stations, 72 trains cars, 18 railway stations, and hundreds of cars and shops.

Responsibility

Bhutto, in a letter to Musharaff written on 16 October 2007, named four persons involved in an alleged plot to kill her. These included the current Intelligence Bureau (IB) Chief Ijaz Shah, former chief minister of Punjab Chaudhry Pervaiz Elahi, Sind Chief Minister Arbab Ghulam Rahim, and the former ISI chief, Hamid Gul.

A *Times* (UK) article names al-Qaeda- and Taliban-backed warlords based in Waziristan and other areas of northwestern Pakistan as likely suspects, but also points to elements within the Pakistani Inter-Services Intelligence with close ties to Islamists as equally likely to have been behind the killing. The article also claims that President Musharraf is unlikely to have ordered the assassination. However, Bhutto herself had emailed Mark Siegel, her U.S. spokesman, lobbyist and friend, in October 2007, saying that because the Musharraf government was not providing adequate security, she would hold Musharraf responsible if she were killed. Mark Siegel had forwarded this email to both U.S. Representative Steve Israel and Wolf Blitzer of CNN with instructions that they publish the email only in the event of Bhutto's death.

On 27 December, al-Qaeda commander Mustafa Abu al-Yazid is said to have claimed responsibility for the assassination, telling Adnkronos International that "They terminated the most precious American asset which vowed to defeat the mujahideen." The article further claims that al-Yazid stated that al-Qaeda second-in-command Ayman al-Zawahiri ordered the killing in October 2007. The *Asia Times Online* also reported that it had received a claim of responsibility from al-Yazid by telephone. U.S. intelligence officials have said that they cannot confirm this claim of responsibility. Nonetheless, U.S. analysts have said that al-Qaeda was a likely, or even prime suspect. For its part, the Pakistani Interior Ministry states that it has proof that al-Qaeda was behind the assassination, stating "that the suicide bomber belonged to Lashkar-e-Jhangvi – an al Qaeda-linked Sunni Muslim militant group that the government has blamed for hundreds of killings". The Interior Ministry also claimed to have intercepted a statement by militant leader Baitullah Mehsud, said to be linked to al-Qaeda, in which he congratulated his followers for carrying out the assassination. On December 29, a Mehsud spokesman told The Associated Press that Mehsud was not at all involved in the assassination: "I strongly deny it. Tribal people have their own customs. We don't strike women. It is a conspiracy by government, military and intelligence agencies." The PPP also called the government's blame of Mehsud a diversion: "The story that al-Qaida or Baitullah Mehsud did it appears to us to be a planted story, an incorrect story, because they want to divert the attention," said Farhatullah Babar, a spokesman for Bhutto's party.

On 30 December, *Scotland on Sunday* quoted MI5 sources saying that factions of Pakistan's Inter-Services Intelligence may be responsible for the assassination. Bhutto anticipated that three senior allies of General Musharraf were out to kill her in a secret email to Foreign Secretary David Miliband written weeks before her death.

Reactions

Pakistani Government

According to state television, Musharraf held an emergency cabinet meeting after he received word of the blast. He addressed the nation, saying that "They shall not rest till we tackle this problem and eliminate all the terrorists. This is the only way the nation will be able to move forward, otherwise this will be the biggest obstacle to their advancement." Pakistani police implored citizens to stay at home; increasing violence and rioting is expected as a direct effect of Bhutto's death.

Mahmud Ali Durrani, the Pakistani ambassador to the United States, called Bhutto's death "a national tragedy," and stated that " we have lost one of their important, very important and, I would stress, liberal leaders."

In a televised address, Pakistan President Pervez Musharraf publicly condemned the killing of Bhutto, proclaiming a three-day mourning with all national flags at half mast.

Opposition

Nawaz Sharif was the first mainstream political leader to reach the hospital and express his solidarity with Bhutto's family and political workers, saying that "I would fight your [Bhutto's] war from now on", that he shared the grief of "the entire nation," and that "it is not a sad day, it is a dark, darkest, gloomiest day in the history of this country. Something unthinkable has happened. Something inconceivable, unthinkable has happened." Despite extreme political enmity between the two leaders during the 1990s, both vowed to introduce politics of tolerance before returning from exile and had earlier signed the Charter of Democracy. After signing the charter, they said that they would work for an end to the rule of General Musharraf. Earlier in the day, Nawaz Sharif's political meeting had also been shot at, resulting in the death of four people. Later that day, Sharif demanded that Musharraf "quit immediately" and said that the Pakistan Muslim League (N), his political party, would boycott the January elections.

Chairman Imran Khan of the Tehreek-e-Insaf party strongly condemned the assassination of Benazir Bhutto. "It is a dastardly act designed to destabilise Pakistan with the government responsible for not providing her security though she was demanding it. They must fight this menace of terrorism. It is a black day in the history of Pakistan and an irreparable loss to this country," Khan said.

PPP president Javaid Manzoor said, "They [Bhutto's supporters] are shocked. They are stunned. Every single one of us is mourning the loss of their leader," also stating that he believed that the next election, scheduled for 8 January would be canceled. PPP senior vice chairman Makhdoom Amin Fahim later called for a 40-day mourning across Pakistan. PPP spokesman Farhatullah Babar said the PPP was unhappy with the government's declaration of the death coming as a result of an accident and said that the PPP wanted to see a change in the direction of the investigation. He called for an independent inquiry into the assassination by international experts. He also said that "had the government accepted their demand of conducting an inquiry into Karachi's 18 October blast by international experts, this incident would not have happened."

Bhutto's Family

Bhutto's husband, Asif Ali Zardari, who flew with their children from Dubai to Islamabad in the wake of his wife's death, said, "All I can say is we're devastated; it's a total shock." Her son, Bilawal Bhutto Zardari, read her instructions on the future of the Pakistan People's Party on December 30. He was appointed Chairman of the Pakistan People's Party on 30 December 2007 in accordance with his mother's wish, and his father will be co-chairman.

International reaction to the assassination of Benazir Bhutto

The international reaction to the assassination of Benazir Bhutto consisted of universal condemnation across the international community.

International Organizations

Al-Qaeda spokesman Mustafa Abu al-Yazid was quoted in Philippine media saying that "we terminated the most precious American asset who vowed to defeat the mujahideen."

However, a spokesman for Al-Qaeda-linked Pakistani militant Baitullah Mehsud was quoted the following day as saying, "I strongly deny it. Tribal people have their own customs. They don't strike women."

Arab League Secretary General Amr Moussa strongly condemned the assassination, saying: "They condemn this assassination and terrorist act, and pray God Almighty to bless her soul."

Commonwealth of Nations Secretary-General Don McKinnon said "I hope that this terrible tragedy will make crystal clear the folly of violence and the importance of restraint and reconciliation as the only way of consolidating the democratic process. The Commonwealth stands by Pakistan in that effort."

European Union – European Commission President José Manuel Barroso condemned the assassination as "an attack against democracy and against Pakistan," and "[hopes] that Pakistan will remain firmly on track for return to democratic civilian rule."

First Vice President Margot Wallström said, "In a region of such global importance, Benazir's was a rare woman's voice speaking out for democracy and against violence. Much of her life was spent working for these values. I am saddened by this loss and send condolences to her family and to the people of Pakistan. I hope that democracy will prevail there and that the country will remain on track for a return to democratic civilian rule."

Organization of the Islamic Conference Secretary General Ekmeleddin Ýhsanoglu "condemned in strongest terms the outrageous and brutal murder of the former Prime Minister of Pakistan and leader of Pakistan People's Party, Ms. Benazir Bhutto in a shocking suicide attack in Rawalpindi."

United Nations Secretary-General Ban Ki-moon said: "I strongly condemn this heinous crime and call for the perpetrators to be brought to justice as soon as possible.

This represents an assault on stability in Pakistan and its democratic processes."

The Security Council held an emergency meeting and unanimously condemned the assassination. World Bank Group President Robert Zoellick said, "This tragedy will only hinder Pakistan's critical agenda of meeting the urgent needs of its many citizens. On behalf of the World Bank Group, I would like to extend my sympathies and deepest condolences to Ms. Bhutto's family and to the families of the other victims of this tragic event."

Non-Governmental Organizations

Amnesty International – Asian Program Director Catherine Baber said: "It is shocking to see someone's life cut short in such a brutal way. Attacks such as these can never be justified. They violate international law and the rules of democratic behaviour. They know that the government of President Musharraf will find itself under enormous pressure to go after the culprits and keep the country calm and stable, but Amnesty International calls on President Musharraf – and on the security forces to exercise restraint and uphold the rule of law. The killing of Benazir Bhutto must not be allowed to become a setback to civilian governance or indeed lead to a further crackdown on civil liberties."

United States Government Relations Director Alex Arriaga said: "Pakistan is at a dangerous crossroads. If it cannot rely on an independent judiciary, some of the most dangerous aspects of martial law will become enshrined in its legal and political system, leaving the people's human rights in the balance. The United States government must press its ally, which has used the 'War on Terror' to justify its actions, and put an end to this slippery slope. Without these steps, the Bush administration will further acquiesce that fundamental rights can be denied, and those who oppose Musharraf are likely to face intimidation – or even death."

Human Rights Watch – A statement was calling the assassination a "tragic event with serious implications for

Pakistan's transition to democracy" and stating that "political violence of this nature has claimed far too many innocent lives in Pakistan and it must stop. Benazir Bhutto was a democrat who believed in the supremacy of constitutional rule and throughout her career sought power through the ballot box. Today, she died campaigning for votes and calling for a free election." HRW South Asia researcher, speaking for the organization, called on the Pakistani government to "undertake an independent and transparent investigation into Bhutto's assassination and fully cooperate with such an investigation."

Africa

Algeria – The Foreign Ministry issued a statement, saying that "Algeria is keen to condemn with the greatest firmness this criminal act, which came to shatter the fate of an exceptional personality, fully involved in the democratic fight for the renewal of her country."

Egypt – Foreign Minister Ahmed Aboul Gheit "conveyed deep condolences to the bereaved family of Benazir Bhutto, her party workers, government and people of Pakistan.."

Liberia – President Ellen Johnson-Sirleaf released a statement, saying that she was "deeply disturbed and saddened by the events in Pakistan."

Libya – The Foreign Ministry released a statement condemning the "odious terrorist operation" and affirming its "staunch opposition to all that is likely to jeopardize security and peace in Pakistani society".

Morocco – King Mohammed VI condemned the assassination in a message to Musharraf, describing Bhutto as "one of illustrious leaders [of Pakistan] both in the Government and in the opposition."

Namibia – A Foreign Affairs Ministry statement called on the Pakistani authorities to "ensure that those who have carried this pre-meditated and cowardly killing are brought to justice." It also offered condolences to the families of Bhutto and those who were killed in the blast.

Nigeria – President Umaru Yar'Adua urged Bhutto's family, the Pakistani government and her supporters "to take solace in the knowledge that she died in active pursuit of her vision of true democracy for her country, and that in death, she has become an eternal martyr to the cause she believed in with all her heart."

South Africa – Foreign Affairs spokesman Ronnie Mamoepa said, "Clearly South Africa is saddened by the news of the murder of Benazir Bhutto and condemns unequivocally this outrageous act of violence. They call on the Pakistani people do everything in their power, to leave no stone unturned to find the perpetrators of this dastardly act."

Tunisia – The Foreign Affairs Ministry released a statement that strongly denounced the assassination, expressing "regret over the Pakistani official's slaying."

Uganda – Foreign Affairs Minister Isaac Musumba said, "It is very deplorable and very pathetic. They thought that democracy was finally having its day in Pakistan. The murder of Bhutto and other people shows that terrorism must continue to be fought relentlessly and without compromise."

Asia

Afghanistan – President Hamid Karzai condemned "the act of cowardice and immense brutality in the strongest possible terms." He praised Bhutto for "having sacrificed her life for the sake of Pakistan and for the sake of this region."

Bahrain – The government denounced the assassination, saying that "[it] extends its sincere condolences to Bhutto's family and all the Pakistani people" and calling for "self-restraint."

Bangladesh – Prime Minister Fakhruddin Ahmed condemned the attack, stating that "it was an unpardonable crime that has shocked the world. The government and people of Bangladesh mourned this tragedy with their Pakistani brethren."

Brunei - Sultan Hassanal Bolkiah "expressed shock" and condemned Bhutto's assassination. He also conveyed his deepest condolences and profound respects to the people of Pakistan and to the family and friends of the late Benazir Bhutto.

Cambodia - Prime Minister Hun Sen condemned the assassination, calling it "coward terrorism", and said that her killing was "a serious problem in Pakistan". He also expressed his condolences to Bhutto's family and called for all political parties in Pakistan to solve matters patiently.

China – A Foreign Ministry spokesperson Qin Gang said that China was "shocked at the killing of Pakistan's opposition leader Benazir Bhutto" and "strongly condemns the terrorist attack."

India – Prime Minister Manmohan Singh said he was "deeply shocked and horrified to hear of the heinous assassination of Mrs. Benazir Bhutto. Mrs. Bhutto was no ordinary political leader, but one who left a deep imprint on her time and age. Her contributions to India–Pakistan relations were exemplary. In her death, the sub-continent has lost an outstanding leader who worked for democracy and reconciliation in her country. The manner of her going is a reminder of the common dangers that their region faces from cowardly acts of terrorism and of the need to eradicate this dangerous threat. My heartfelt condolences go to her family and the people of Pakistan who have suffered a grievous blow."

Foreign Minister Pranab Mukherjee said he "heard with shock and horror of the death of Mrs. Benazir Bhutto," whose "contributions to democracy, to the improvement of India–Pakistan relations, and to the restoration of normalcy within Pakistan will be an inspiration. Mrs. Bhutto was a brave and outstanding woman leader of the sub-continent. That she should fall to a barbarous terrorist attack is particularly tragic, and should strengthen their resolve to fight this scourge."

Indonesia – President Susilo Bambang Yudhoyono said, "...he was shocked and condemned the terrorists". He expressed a hope that such a fatal accident will not harm democracy in Pakistan, which is now unstable especially towards its general elections which will be held on January 15, 2008. He also said that "the incident had dealt a serious blow to the transition of democracy."

Iran – Foreign Minister Manouchehr Mottaki expressed the deep sympathy of the Iranian nation and government and said he hoped that the Pakistani government would try and track down the culprits behind this crime against Bhutto and a number of innocent people who were present at the scene when a gunman fatally shot her and set off a bomb. A Foreign Affairs Ministry spokesman Mohammad Ali Hosseini said that "we hope the Pakistani government will identify and bring to justice those behind such a criminal act and restore tranquility in the country," and that "the Pakistan government should use all efforts to identify the terrorist group which caused this incident and punish them to prevent terrorist groups from finding opportunities to undertake such actions again."

Iraq – President Jalal Talabani called on the world to unite against the "cancer of terrorism".

Israel – President Shimon Peres praised Bhutto, saying "[she] was a brave woman who did not conceal her opinions, knew no fear, and served her nation with unusual bravery and ability. She was an immeasurably charismatic leader and a warrior for peace in her land and all the world." President Peres hailed Bhutto as a "courageous woman" and said he was "shocked" by the news of her assassination.

Deputy and Foreign Affairs Minister Tzipi Livni issued the following statement: "They convey their condolences to the people of Pakistan and to the families of the victims. Benazir Bhutto was a well-known leader in Pakistan and in the international community who demonstrated brave leadership for her people. Israel expresses the hope that Pakistan will continue along the path of reconciliation, moderation and democracy."

Ambassador to the United Nations Dan Gillerman said that in the weeks prior to her assassination, Bhutto had expressed fear of being killed by extremist elements in Pakistan in emails she sent to him.

Japan – Foreign Affairs Minister Masahiko Kômura condemned the attack, saying that "it is absolutely unacceptable to try to solve something by the means of violence."

Jordan – King Abdullah II, in a message to Musharraf, condemned the assassination and expressed Jordan's "support to Pakistan" to overcome the consequences of this incident.

Kuwait – Cabinet Affairs Minister Faisal Mohammad Al-Hajji said, "The State of Kuwait strongly condemns the vicious terrorist act which targeted the convoy of Mrs. Benazir Bhutto", and also said that Kuwait expresses sympathies for the families of Bhutto and all those who were killed.

Lebanon – Prime Minister Fouad Siniora said that "Lebanon was shocked by the news of the assassination of former Prime Minister and leader of the Pakistan People's Party Ms. Benazir Bhutto", adding that "on behalf of the Lebanese people we denounce, condemn and deplore the assassination."

Malaysia – Prime Minister Abdullah Ahmad Badawi extended his deepest condolences to the families of Bhutto and the others who were killed. He also said, "The resort to extremism and violence is unacceptable and cannot be tolerated anywhere at any time. The perpetrators must be brought to justice." He added, "I hope the people in Pakistan will remain calm and I pray that the situation in Pakistan will soon stabilise."

Nepal – Prime Minister Girija Prasad Koirala said he was "shocked to hear the murder of Bhutto."

Philippines – President Gloria Macapagal-Arroyo condemned the assassination, saying "They mourn with the nation of Pakistan over the deaths of Benazir Bhutto and others killed in the shooting and bomb attack in Rawalpindi. They strongly condemn this unmitigated, senseless atrocity, even as we convey our sympathies to the followers of former Prime Minister Bhutto and the families of those who perished. Whoever perpetrated it, this attack is an assault on democracy. The Philippines joins hands with the entire civilized world in solidarity against such mindless barbarity and in unwavering defense of peace, freedom, law and order." Arroyo called on the international community to join hands in preserving peace and order and democracy.

Saudi Arabia – King Abdullah stated that the assassins were "wicked murderers who are distant from Islam and morals."

Singapore – The Foreign Affairs Ministry released a statement saying that Singapore "is shocked and horrified at the suicide bomb attack" and strongly condemns the murders.

The heads of state and government also sent condolence letters to Bhutto's family.

South Korea – A Foreign Ministry statement said: "The (South Korean) government cannot hide its bitter shock over the death of former Pakistani Prime Minister Benazir Bhutto, who was killed by terrorists while on an election campaign, and it offers its sincerest condolences to the family of the deceased. Our government condemns any type of terrorist acts."

Sri Lanka – A Foreign Affairs Ministry statement described Bhutto as a South Asian leader who "successfully stood up for democracy", adding that "this brutal assassination underlines the need for the absolute commitment to fight against terrorism in all its forms and manifestations, in order to make it unacceptable in civilized society."

Syria – A Government spokesman said, "The Syrian government and people...express sincere condolences to the family of Ms. Bhutto, the Pakistan People's Party and the Pakistani government and the confidence that Pakistan will be able to overcome the difficult conditions."

Thailand – Prime Minister Surayud Chulanont condemned the assassination of Pakistani opposition leader Benazir Bhutto, branding the act as deplorable.

A statement issued by Foreign Ministry Spokesman Tharit Charungvat said, "Thailand was deeply shocked and saddened by the deplorable act which led to the deaths of Mrs Benazir Bhutto and several other innocent bystanders. Thailand condemns all forms of terrorist and extremist acts and calls on all parties to react with restraint and work together for the stability of Pakistan."

Turkey – Prime Minister Recep Tayyip Erdoðan expressed his sorrow over Bhutto's demise during a phone conversation with Musharraf. Erdoðan, who strongly condemned the terrorist attack, also said that he hoped such attack would not hamper the democratization process in Pakistan.

President Abdullah Gül, who met Bhutto during a visit to Pakistan earlier that month, called on the international community to assist Pakistan in this "critical" time as it prepares for parliamentary elections. Gul said: "They should own up to their country and make sure there is no more bloodshed".

United Arab Emirates – Foreign Affairs Minister Abdallah Bin Zayid Al Nahyan stated: "The UAE has been tormented by this huge loss which did not hit Pakistan only, but also affected the UAE."

Vietnam – The Foreign Affairs Ministry released a statement saying that Vietnam "strongly condemns the brutal terrorist attack" and "hope that...the instigators will be severely punished".

Yemen – A Government official called the assassination a "sinful attack" and "strongly condemned this distressing terrorist act, which was intended to destabilize the security of Pakistan and its national unity."

Europe

Albania – The Foreign Ministry said, "Albania expresses its deepest regret and shock at the tragic event in Pakistan, and strongly condemns this hideous terrorist act".

Austria – Foreign Minister Ursula Plassnik was "shocked and disgusted" by the murder of Benazir Bhutto. Adding that Pakistan "lost a courageous fighter for the country's return to a pluralist democracy."

Azerbaijan – President Ilham Aliyev said, "This tragic event confirms once again the need for mobilization of all forces in order to fight terrorism and for joint efforts against this calamity, which is a source of constant threat to humankind" and expressed his "deepest condolences to the people of Pakistan, as well as to the families of those killed."

Belgium – Prime Minister Guy Verhofstadt said, "This is not only an attack on the life of a former prime minister and present opposition leader. This is yet another attack on the democratic process in Pakistan."

Foreign Minister Karel De Gucht issued a similar condemnation, saying that, "extreme forces are strengthening their actions to destabilize the country and put it into chaos."

Belarus - President Alexander Lukashenko expressed his condolences to the people of Pakistan, President Musharraf, and to the families of those who were killed. President Lukashenko Described the incident as a terrorist attack that took the life of the "well-known policy maker" Benazir Bhutto.

Bulgaria – A Foreign Ministry statement has strongly condemned the the terrorist act and said "Bulgaria extended its deepest condolences to Bhutto's family."

Croatia – President Stjepan Mesic has condemned the killing of Pakistan opposition leader Benazir Bhutto, stating, "terrorism is one of the greatest evils the modern world is faced with and which should be battled with joint efforts".

Czech Republic – Prime Minister Mirek Topolánek sharply denounced the attack, saying he "hopes the crime will not trigger an avalanche of further violent acts."

President Vaclav Klaus said the hatred behind the attack is a "threat to civilization".

Denmark – Foreign Minister Per Stig Møller said: "It is terrible and a tragedy for Pakistani society, because there was a real hope of reforms and democratization conjoined with her return to Pakistan and with the election on January 8. It is also an attack against that process, as the people who did this do not want reforms and democracy."

Finland – Prime Minister Matti Vanhanen said, "Benazir Bhutto made a brave return to her homeland to take part in free elections and to promote democracy. Her tragic death is a setback to democracy and speaks in a shocking way about the internal confrontations of Pakistan."

France – President Nicolas Sarkozy "condemned the odious act with the greatest severity," stating that "terrorism and violence have no place in the democratic debate and in the combat of ideas and programmes. More than ever it is necessary for the [Pakistani] legislative elections to take place in conditions of pluralism, transparency and security."

Foreign Affairs Minister Bernard Kouchner referred to the assassination as an "odious act" that "reaffirms France's commitment to the stability of Pakistan and its democracy."

Germany – Chancellor Angela Merkel stated that the "cowardly act underscored the need to continue the fight against terrorism and support those who suffer its consequences"

Foreign Minister Frank-Walter Steinmeier commented that Bhutto's death was a "severe blow to everyone in Pakistan who is fighting for democracy".

Greece – Foreign Minister Dora Bakoyannis said, "Greece condemns the terrorist attack in the most categorical way that, just two weeks ahead of the Parliamentary elections in Pakistan, has led to this tragic loss." She called Bhutto "a leading international personality who struggled steadfastly for democracy, peace, respect for human dignity and reconciliation in her country," and stated that "we are watching the events with great concern, at the same time expressing the wish and the hope that this country will follow the path towards the construction of a democratic regime. This will also constitute the sole vindication of the tragic sacrifice of Benazir Bhutto."

Hungary – Foreign Affairs Ministry spokesman Lajos Szelestey said, "Hungary strongly condemns all forms of terrorism". He called the attack which resulted in the murder of Bhutto and dozens of others "an unjustifiable crime, which will seriously hamper the democratization process of Pakistan and will render the elections in January more difficult".

Iceland – President Ólafur Ragnar Grímsson said Bhutto was "an admired leader that warned against terrorism and extremists' views, highly educated and broadminded, full of energy."

Ireland – Describing herself as "shocked and saddened," President Mary McAleese said, "On my own behalf and on behalf of the people of Ireland, I send my deepest condolences to her family and to the people of Pakistan and especially to those members of the Pakistan community here in Ireland."

Prime Minister Bertie Ahern said, "Ms Bhutto and her party have been campaigning heavily in the run-up to the parliamentary elections due to be held in less than two weeks, an election which will provide all the people of Pakistan with an opportunity to secure democracy for their country. It is my sincere hope that this appalling attack will not prevent the Pakistani people from achieving that objective."

Foreign Affairs Minister Dermot Ahern said he was "...deeply shocked by the assassination". He also called upon the Pakistani authorities to do their utmost to ensure that Pakistan continues on its path back to democracy.

Italy – Prime Minister Romano Prodi said, in a statement, "I express my sadness and that of the whole government following the tragic death of Benazir Bhutto, a woman who wanted to fight her battle until the end with just one weapon that of dialogue and political discussion. I condemn with great indignation the blind rage of terror which has again seen blood spilled and brought pain to Pakistan, a country already too often martyred by fanaticism.

The difficult path towards peace and democracy in this region should not be abandoned and the sacrifice of the former prime minister should be the strongest example for those who do not give up in the face of terrorism."

Foreign Affairs Minister Massimo D'Alema said, "I absolutely condemn this barbaric act of violence which, in striking at Pakistan just days before elections, places serious question marks against the complex and difficult path towards democracy."

Luxembourg – Prime Minister Jean-Claude Juncker described the assassination as a "deeply contemptible act."

Malta – Foreign Minister Michael Frendo said, "The killing of Benazir Bhutto is an attack on democracy and on secular politics in Pakistan. They express their solidarity with the people of Pakistan at this moment of loss."

Netherlands – Foreign Affairs Minister Maxime Verhagen expressed his disgust over the bombing. On behalf of the Dutch Cabinet, he stated the bomb attack is a huge blow for the restoration of democracy in Pakistan.

Norway – Prime Minister Jens Stoltenberg said, "It is with sadness that we have received the news of the murder of the former Prime Minister. They condemn the attack as a serious atrocity against the process of reestablishing democracy in Pakistan. Bhutto was a controversial, but a brave to reestablish the democracy in Pakistan, and she was in the middle of the process when she was killed. Her death is a terrible blow on this process." He also said it was important that "the despicable act would not halt the reforms in Pakistan."

Poland – Foreign Minister Radosaw Sikorski condemned the assassination and added that he hopes that killing will not affect next year's elections.

Portugal – President Anibal Cavaco Silva condemned the "tragic attacks" that killed the former Pakistani prime minister Benazir Bhutto, describing the killing as a "heinous act". He also expressed "deep sorrow and solidarity" to the president and people of Pakistan.

Russia – The Foreign Affairs Ministry "firmly condemned" the attack, "expressed [their] condolences to Benazir Bhutto's relatives and loved ones" and "hoped that the Pakistani leadership will manage to take necessary steps to ensure stability in the country."

In a statement addressed to Pervez Musharraf, President Vladimir Putin expressed his condolences to friends and relatives of the victims as well as hope that the perpetrators will be found and punished. He also commented that "forces of terrorism are challenging not only Pakistan, but the international community".

Spain – Prime Minister José Luis Rodríguez Zapatero said: "I want to express the most firm condemnation at the savage terrorist attack carried out in Rawalpindi."

Sweden – Foreign Minister Carl Bildt said in a press conference about an hour after the murder that he felt both disgusted and angry for what had happened, and also worried over the further consequences.

Switzerland – The Foreign Affairs Ministry released a statement strongly condemning the attack. It called on Pakistani authorities and all concerned actors to maintain the country's stability and to continue pursuing the democratic process.

Ukraine – Speaker of Parliament Arseniy Yatsenyuk, after the parliament had held a minute's silence, stated that Parliament "wished to extend its condolences to the family of the deceased (Bhutto), and to the Pakistani people for their loss." Ukraine's Foreign Ministry called for an objective and detailed investigation of the assassination of Pakistan's opposition leader Benazir Bhutto.

United Kingdom – Prime Minister Gordon Brown stated, "Benazir Bhutto may have been killed by terrorists but the terrorists must not be allowed to kill democracy in Pakistan and this atrocity strengthens their resolve that terrorists will not win there, here or anywhere in the world." Brown further stated those responsible were "cowards, afraid of democracy" and that the British government would "work with all in the Pakistani community in Britain and elsewhere in the world, so that we can have a peaceful, safe, and democratic Pakistan."

Foreign Secretary David Miliband released a statement saying, "In targeting Benazir Bhutto, extremist groups have in their sights all those committed to democratic processes in Pakistan. They cannot and must not succeed. This is a time for restraint but also unity," also stating that he was "deeply shocked."

Justice Secretary Jack Straw added in his statement, "The sense of grief at her senseless killing will I know be shared not just by Pakistani communities across the world but by everyone, because this terrorism is an attack on us all, regardless of race, religion or party. They will ensure that it is defeated."

Vatican City – Secretary of State Tarcisio Bertone expressed the sadness of Pope Benedict XVI, saying that "the Holy Father expresses sentiments of deep sympathy and spiritual closeness to the members of her family and to the entire Pakistani nation. He prays that further violence will be avoided and that every effort will be made to build a climate of respect and trust, which are so necessary if good order is to be maintained in society and if the country's political institutions are to operate effectively."

Spokesman Federico Lombardi said that "this attack shows how extremely difficult it is to pacify a nation so wrought by violence." He also said that the Vatican "share[s] the sadness of the Pakistani population."

North America

Bahamas – Prime Minister Hubert Ingraham said, "Her assassination has left much of the world in a state of shock and grave concern for the future of Pakistan, the region and the world."

Canada – Foreign Affairs Minister Maxime Bernier issued the statement: "Canada condemns in the strongest terms this attack on the restoration of Pakistan's efforts to return to full democracy. Today's violence is especially heinous in view of the upcoming elections on January 8, 2008. The anti-democratic intent of the perpetrators could not be more obvious. I urge the Government and people of Pakistan to continue to reject all forms of violence and to resist those who seek to destabilize their country. Stability in Pakistan is vital for regional stability and security. We extend our deepest condolences to the family of Benazir Bhutto, to the families of the other victims of today's attack, and to the Pakistani people. Our thoughts are with them at this difficult time."

Prime Minister Stephen Harper later added to reporters at a press meeting in Calgary: "We condemn this attack in the strongest possible terms. This was an abhorrent act of terror. We hope that the government of Pakistan will act to bring the perpetrators to justice".

Jamaica – Prime Minister Bruce Golding expressed shock and outrage at the assassination and expressed the hope that "the Pakistani people will find lasting peace within a framework of democracy, tolerance and mutual respect."

Mexico – Foreign Affairs Secretary Patricia Espinosa "energetically condemned" the event, reaffirmed Mexico's rejection of "terrorism in all its forms and the loss of innocent poeple's lives", and expressed their "deepest condolences to Benazir Bhutto's relatives and the families of the 20 other victims, as well as to the people and authorities of Pakistan."

Trinidad and Tobago – The Foreign Affairs Ministry released a statement, saying that "the Government and people of the Republic of Trinidad and Tobago express the deepest sympathy to the Government and people of the Islamic Republic of Pakistan and family members of former Prime Minister Ms Benazir Bhutto, political leader of the Pakistan People's Party, on the tragic incident which resulted in her untimely demise and that of innocent civilians", adding that "the Government of the Republic of Trinidad and Tobago strongly condemns this act and reaffirms its unwavering commitment to international efforts to eradicate terrorism."

United States – President George Bush strongly condemned the assassination, urging her killers to be brought to justice. Bush condemned the assassination as a "cowardly act by murderous extremists," and encouraged Pakistan to "honor Benazir Bhutto's memory by continuing with the democratic process for which she so bravely gave her life." Bush also offered some strong praise of Bhutto, noting that "she knew that her return to Pakistan earlier this year put her life at risk. Yet she refused to let assassins to dictate the course of her country."

Speaker of the House Nancy Pelosi said, "The brutal assassination of former Pakistani Prime Minister Benazir Bhutto is a tragic setback for the restoration of democracy in Pakistan. Her courageous return to Pakistan this year gave hope to all those concerned by efforts to extinguish rule of law there."

Senate Majority Leader Harry Reid said, "It is important, when faced with the violence and loss of innocent life over the last few days, that political leaders show a commitment to resolve but also restraint. Extremists must be brought to justice, but extremism must not undermine commitment to the rule of law, to human rights, and to democracy."

At another press briefing at around 13:00 EST on December 27, a State Department spokesman asserted that "some kind of postponement or delay" in Pakistan's democratic process would be "a victory" for "the extremists" who were responsible for Benazir Bhutto's assassination. He also asserted that "perhaps the best antidote to extremism is the continuation of the democratic process." He called for a "credible and transparent" investigation of the attack, and alluded to the "broad international outrage" about the incident.

Ambassador to the United Nations Zalmay Khalilzad, while describing Bhutto as a "courageous figure", said that "The world has much at stake in the success of Pakistan's democratic institutions. It's a great tragedy because she stood for moderation, for rule of law, for democracy in her country, and her death is a loss for the cause of moderation, democracy, and rule of law for Pakistan. She was clear-headed about the problems of her country, the challenges that she faced — even the security challenges she faced."

Oceania

Australia – Prime Minister Kevin Rudd urged restraint, saying "Benazir Bhutto showed great courage and defiance in her resistance to extremism. I urge all parties in Pakistan to act with restraint and to work for a return to a peaceful democratic process. It is my hope that a democratic Pakistan will be Benazir Bhutto's legacy."

Fiji – Finance Minister Mahendra Chaudhry said, "Ms. Bhutto was, in recent times, a beacon of hope for the millions of Pakistani people who aspired for a free, fair and democratic Pakistan. It is a real tragedy that Ms Bhutto has not been allowed to realise her vision for Pakistan and the rest of the world."

New Zealand – Prime Minister Helen Clark said she was deeply shocked and saddened saying "Benazir Bhutto showed great courage in returning to Pakistan to contest the election. She had survived attempts on her life and was acutely aware of the dangers she faced in returning to campaign for the elections. Her death is a great loss to Pakistan and to the region. My sympathies go out to her immediate family, political colleagues, and to the people of Pakistan for their terrible loss."

South America

Argentina – President Cristina Fernández de Kirchner condemned "energetically the awful attack that (...) took the life of Benazir Bhutto. The Argentine government wishes to express its deepest condolences to the Bhutto family, as well to the other victims' families and the whole people of Pakistan".

Brazil – President Luiz Inacio Lula da Silva condemned the attacks and spoke of his "great pain and indignation" at the violence. Later, in a statement, Lula da Silva reaffirmed his "firm rejection to the use of violence in political life" and extended his condolences "to the families of the victims and the Pakistani nation" in the name of the Brazilian Government.

Chile – The Foreign Affairs Ministry expressed deep consternation at the loss of Bhutto and condemned the events as "terrorist acts." The ministry also expressed its hope that "this event does not dim the opening process towards a total democracy and the national reconciliation."

Guyana – The Foreign Affairs Ministry sent an official message conveying the condolences of the government and people of Guyana and hoped "peace and stability will prevail."

Paraguay – The Foreign Affairs Ministry issued a statement expressing its rejection of "acts of violence and the loss of human life", repudiating "acts of terrorism in any of its manifestations", and "[sending] to the Bhutto family, to the families of other victims, as well as to the people and authorities of Pakistan, its sincere condolences."

Peru – President Alan García stated that "Peru reaffirms its absolute opposition to terrorism, which must firmly be fought with total respect to human rights and democratic liberties." Garcia expressed the condolences of the Peruvian people to Bhutto's family and hoped that Pakistan would soon find order. It was also revealed that García was a close friend of Bhutto, according to a Chancellorship note.

Venezuela – President Hugo Chavez said, "We received the news with great pain, and I hope this is never repeated ever again, anywhere."

2

Hanging of Zulfikar Ali Bhutto and Her Tryst with Destiny

During the summer of 1977, each of the four Bhutto children returned to Pakistan from various points in the world. They met at their father's official residence, a white mansion set in beautiful grounds in Rawalpindi, near Islamabad.

When Benazir stepped off the airplane in Islamabad and into the arms of her father, he said, "Thank God you've completed your education and are home. Now you can help me." Those were the words Benazir wanted to hear. She was now ready to work for her country.

Within a matter of days, Benazir moved into a small office near her father's at the secretariat and began sorting through his files. Considering her education, she was starting in a lowly position. Yet she felt useful and ready to learn as much as she could about the government and her father's political responsibilities.

What seemed like an ideal beginning to her career was about to be destroyed. On the night of July 7, 1977, the Rawalpindi household was suddenly shaken out of a quiet steep.

"Wake up! Get dressed! Hurry!" Benazir remembers her mother warning. "The army's taken over!"

In a state of fear, Benazir ran to her parents to find out what was happening. Nusrat said that a coup d'etat, or overthrow of the government, by General Zia had taken place.

While Nusrat explained their situation to the rest of 'he family, Zulfikar Ali Bhutto contacted General Zia. The General said that he intended to hold another election in ninety days, and that Ali Bhutto was under house arrest. An official car was on its way to the house to take Ali Bhutto to his place of detention.

Shocked by the news, Ali Bhutto thought of his family. He instructed Nusrat and the children to return to the family name in Karachi. Benazir's mother suggested the two boys, Shah and Mir, leave immediately, and perhaps even leave Pakistan. They might be in danger as the sons of the arrested prime minister.

The Bhuttos waited for Zia to come and take the prime minister away. During the long delay, they packed their things. The tense atmosphere was broken by a sharp cry from Nusrat Bhutto. When Benazir and her siblings ran downstairs, they saw Ali Bhutto looking out of the window of a black Mercedes. He was trying to say good-bye. He was soon out of range as the car disappeared through the gates.

The comfortable, safe life of Benazir Bhutto was suddenly in danger. As she stood and watched the car disappear from sight, she recalled the last conversation she had had with her father that evening. He had asked if she believed General Zia would actually hold elections in ninety days as he promised.

"Yes, he will," she had said without hesitation. Her father had called her naive, and explained in harsh words that a government seized by the army did not promise much future for democracy. Zia had ignored the constitution of 1973, and Ali Bhutto thought Zia would not give up power easily.

General Zia had promised Bhutto he could stay anywhere he desired. This was not the case, however. Bhutto wanted to go to his home in Larkana. Instead, Zia sent him to the colonial rest house in, the jagged hills of Murree, where the Bhutto family had spent many vacations. Zia believed that this faraway location would keep Bhutto out of politics. Despite these moves by the new government, both Ali Bhutto and the PPP remained popular.

With General Zia in control of the country, a kind of religious extremism was practised. During the month of Ramadan, Muslims are not allowed, according to their religion, to eat or drink in public between sunrise and sunset. Normally, if a Muslim breaks this rule, he or she is seen as unfaithful. Zia, though, threatened to arrest and punish. anyone who broke their fast.

As expected, the Bhutto family was under a great strain at this time. But for Benazir, at least, this experience prepared her for situations she had not encountered before. One lesson she learned was how to deal with journalists. They called the Karachi home constantly for information about her father. Ali Bhutto simply said, "Invite them all to tea."

Following his advice, Benazir asked an eager group of reporters into the crowded dining room, attempting to correct the many runs romours that were spreading around Karachi and elsewhere. There was even one romour that said Ali Bhutto was responsible for the summer rains that were drowning and damaging the farm crops. Another romour accused Benazir Bhutto of carrying a video camera in her handbag to film illegal political meetings.

During the press conference, Benazir tried to answer as many questions as she could. Later, when talking with her father, she told him of me silly romour she had heard. He advised her to go immediately to the city of Lahore, where most of the people had suffered ruined crops. This would be a good political move to show that the Bhuttos cared.

Benazir was frightened by his suggestion at first. Yet when she and her brother finally went to Lahore, they were surprised at the overwhelming reception they were given. At one point, Ali Bhutto himself telephoned a public meeting in the city to express his sympathy to all those who had lost crops in the flood.

Because of Ali Bhutto's continued popularity while still in captivity, General Zia decided to release him. The Bhutto family was reunited in Karachi. As happy as Benazir was at their father's freedom, she openly expressed her feelings against Zia. Her father spoke sharply to her about this.

He believed everything they said in their house was being recorded. "You are careless," he told his daughter. "You are not in a democracy of the West now.

The excitement at Bhutto's release was soon overshadowed by Zia's attempts to jail Bhutto again on a false accusation. Benazir was caught in the middle of one of these plots before dawn on a September night in 1977. Five men in white suddenly forced open her bedroom door at the Karachi home and pointed machine guns at her. Not only did they threaten her, but they smashed everything in her room.

Meanwhile, Ali Bhutto was escorted out of the house to military headquarters. Benazir dressed quickly and went with him, despite their attempts to leave her behind. She spoke bravely in her father's defense, but, once again, Ali Bhutto was placed in jail. The judge, however, could not find enough evidence to find him guilty, and Ali Bhutto was set free.

Ali Bhutto was eager to return to campaigning. He warned Benazir again about speaking against Zia when she said, "You're going to win the elections and try General Zia for treason." Since he had told her before about the electronic "bugs," this outburst angered him.

Unfortunately, Ali Bhutto's problems were not over. He was again seized by the army and taken from his house in Larkana. He was put in Sukkur Jail briefly before being moved to Karachi Central Jail, and then to Lahore.

While Ali Bhutto was being, moved from jail to jail, Nusrat Bhutto campaigned as a candidate, to replace her husband. Such a step is traditional for political families in Asia. Benazir, too, found herself thrust on stage to give speeches. Although frightened by the crowds, she used everything she had learned at Oxford and tried to hide her fear.

Threatened by the popular response to the Bhutto women, Zia placed Benazir under house arrest for fifteen days. Nusrat Bhutto continued to speak out in public, now saying, "My daughter is used to wearing jewellery. Now she will be proud to wear the chains of imprisonment."

During the time she was under house arrest, Benazir burned most of the Bhutto family photos. She did not want the army to find there and use them in any way.

When she was released, Benazir and Nusrat rented a house in Lahore to be near Ali Bhutto during his trial. Benazir became frustrated and angry by the things she heard. The only response and comfort were the words from her father. "You can imprison a man, but not an idea."

Further arrests and detentions (being held by the police) awaited Benazir and Nusrat during the trial. At one point, Zia ordered the massacre of any people who supported Bhutto. While facing these hardships, both England and America seemed very far away to young Benazir. All she could do was worry behind the walls of her Karachi home.

At the moment, her father was found guilty of murder and sentenced to death. Benazir used her wits to find ways to see him in the Rawalpindi District Jail, and her mother in Lahore. She managed to smuggle messages from Ali Bhutto out of his jail. The messages usually contained advice on how to protest legally against her detention. This advice was rewarded when Benazir was released. Soon after this, though, she had an operation to cure a painful ear infection.

While she was recovering, Benazir's twenty-fifth birthday arrived. To celebrate, she and her mother went to Ali Bhutto's jail. There, Benazir found her father in good spirits, though much thinner than the last time she had seen him. Despite the annoying insects and crawling lizards in the cell, her father teased her and said, "You are twenty-five now and eligible for office." They looked at each other and laughed.

Benazir had decided it was up to her to prepare a legal case to defend her father against the death sentence. To cope with the piles of legal documents, she asked her Oxford friend, Victoria Schofield, to come to Pakistan to help h

In February 1979, Ali Bhutto petitioned a plea in the court to remove his death sentence. The plea was denied. Bhutto was sent back to jail despite messages from Great Britain, the United States, and Saudi Arabia on his behalf.

On April 3, 1979, Benazir and her mother were taken to see Ali Bhutto for the last time in the compound of the Rawalpindi Jail. Through the iron bars, the three of them had only thirty minutes to say their good-byes. His last words to Benazir were, "You don't know how much I love you, how much I've always loved you. You are my jewel. You always have been."

The government reported that on April 4, 1979 (Ali Bhutto was hanged. Benazir, however, believes he may have been killed in some other way because there were no hanging marks on his neck. The real truth may never be known. As a part of Muslim tradition, Nusrat Bhutto began four months of private mourning. The military would not bother Nusrat, but what of Benazir? She did not know what would happen to her. Whatever it was, she decided she would never give up her father's ideals (or his political cause.

Under heavy guard, Benazir and Nusrat Bhutto were taken to the family burial ground in Larkana to pay their final respects to Ali Bhutto. The grave was only a mound of mud without any identification. Through their tears, the women scattered flower petals over the freshly shoveled mud.

Benazir felt stronger after this emotional event. Everything her father had taught her took on new meaning. "Stand up to the challenge. Fight against overwhelming odds. Overrun the enemy. What you make of your destinies is up to you." These were just a few of his words of advice.

Not long after their visit to the grave and their return to jail, mother and daughter were allowed to go to their home in Karachi. Both women were relieved to be home, where they could once again smell the welcome sea breezes.

With the public mourners for Ali Bhutto crowding into the gardens at 70 Clifton, Benazir began to think, about, how she could carry out her father's mission. She turned the house into the business headquarters for the PPP. Here,

Benazir personally conducted meetings for the party from early in the morning until deep into the night. Party members respected the Bhutto name, so they felt satisfied with Benazir leading the party.

The PPP's efforts to win local elections throughout the country were successful, but the national election against Zia was their main focus. They decided to oppose Zia even without Ali Bhutto. This constant threat of opposition forced Zia to cancel the scheduled elections.

Angry at the continued support for the PPP, Zia moved the Bhutto women to Larkana in 1980 and put them under strict house arrest for six months. This was the seventh time Benazir had been arrested in two years. Although this imprisonment was at Al-Murtaza, they were not allowed to have visitors or to talk on the telephone. Also, any mention of the Bhuttos in newspapers was forbidden by the government. The Bhutto family was still a powerful force in Pakistan. Zia hoped that if their names were not mentioned, people would forget about them.

Within the walls of Al-Murtaza, boredom was Benazir's biggest enemy. Nusrat and Benazir's only contact with the outside world was a shortwave radio that received broadcasts from the British Broadcasting Corporation (BBC). In December 1979, when they heard that Pakistan's neighbour, Afghanistan, had been invaded by the Soviet Army, Benazir was stunned. This news deepened her worry about her two brothers. When they had fled Pakistan at the time of the coup, they moved to Afghanistan.

Added tó these worries and the increasing boredom, Benazir and Nusrat were facing the first anniversary of Ali Bhutto's death. Their request to visit his grave was denied.

Benazir needed something to keep her busy. She decided to turn all her energies to challenging 'her six-month detention in court, Her study of law at Oxford, and her father's legal advice in the past, gave her the necessary courage. Benazir and Nusrat were soon free and on their way back to Karachi. Without wasting any time, Benazir became involved in the PPP again. This time, though, Zia's intelligence force followed her and watched her every move.

Benazir continued to have serious problems with her ear, which, interfered with her political work. She worried about the possibility of deafness. To help Benazir recover, Nusrat suggested her daughter go back to Larkana and take over the running of the family farm. It had been seriously neglected since the coup d'etat almost two years before.

For a woman in Pakistan, this assignment was remarkable. But Benazir had little choice: her father was dead, and her brothers were both hiding in Afghanistan. No Bhutto male could do it. So, Benazir travelled to Larkana and took on a landowner's responsibility. She covered every inch of the flat stretches of land with a jeep and supervised the acres of paddy and sugarcane fields.

Benazir's physical and mental problems lessened with these new chores. The people who worked for her had not been managed by a Bhutto family member for two years. Under her direction, the farm prospered. Moreover, Benazir was learning firsthand about the problems faced by the farmers.

At the end of a long day in the fields, Benazir refused to relax. Her evenings were filled with visitors who brought news from the political world, and students who came to speak with her. Many dealt with her as an equal, and she felt she was one of them. Because of her position as a landowner, villagers, too, came to her to settle their personal and marital problems. She disliked making decisions for a married couple, and this was the least favourite part of her job.

Meanwhile, the government was becoming even more strict. Freedom of the press was limited, and political activists were arrested. Nusrat decided the only way to beat Zia in 1980 was for the PPP to unite with a certain section of the opposition party, the PNA. When the two groups came together for discussions, the meeting lasted seven hours. The outcome was called the Movement to Restore Democracy, or the MRD.

Having become very cautious since her father's murder, Benazir distrusted this new organization. But people throughout Pakistan supported the MRD.

The MRD, as well as the continued opposition to his rule, threatened Zia's government. Police broke up a secret meeting of the MRD in the northern part of Punjab Province. There, Nusrat was arrested and sent back to Karachi.

Benazir and her mother had made an agreement that the two of them would never appear at the same meeting together. After their last detention, Nusrat had said, "There is no use in both of us landing in jail again at the same time, so you keep a low political profile. That way, one of us... can stay on the outside to lead the party."

The military rulers were becoming increasingly frustrated with the MRD and the Bhuttos for encouraging the strikes across the country. On March 7, 1981, police searched for Benazir in Karachi all night and the next day. They even invaded the homes of some of Benazir's closest friends. Some were just questioned, and others were put under house arrest.

On this particular right Benazir was staying at a friend's house while Nusrat held a political meeting at 70 Clifton. In the middle of it, the police forced their way in and arrested Nusrat, demanding to know where Benazir was staying. She would not tell them.

As they searched throughout Karachi, the police located Benazir the next day at the home of Nusrat Bhutto's doctor. Benazir was later to learn that Zia had not only arrested her, but six thousand MRD supporters as well.

Not knowing what would happen to her, Benazir was sent to Karachi Central Jail. Five hours later, she learned that her own mother had been placed in a cell without any running water or bedding.

Benazir was kept five days in this jail. On March 13, 1981, in an attempt to frighten her, the police drove her through Karachi to the airport with the sounds of screaming sirens. She was put on an airplane without any explanation as to why and where she was going. On board, she was given a newspaper to read. One of the articles reported that a Pakistani airplane had been hijacked in Afghanistan, and the hijackers were demanding the release of fifty-five

Pakistani political prisoners. One military man and one passenger were shot before the plane was forced to fly to Syria. The article suggested her brother Mir had planned the hijacking. Terrified, Benazir finally understood why she and her mother were being treated as they were. General Zia and the military thought the Bhutto women were involved in planning the hijacking.

Benazir was flown out of Karachi to Sukkur Jail, far away in the Thar Desert. Here, her cell seemed more like a cage, with barred doors on two sides and barred windows on four sides. At night, there was no electricity, and she shivered as the cold winds swept across the desert and whipped through the open bars of her cell. Without blankets or warm clothing, the cold bothered her, making it hard to sleep on the rope cot.

Being separated from people and other prisoners made her feel ill and depressed. She decided she must find things to do to keep herself occupied. Everything Benazir did, from brushing her hair to brushing her teeth, had a set routine. This way, each moment of the day had a purpose.

Benazir did not like the prison food. She was given watery soup and tea with some bread. Sometimes, the guards offered her pumpkin or fish. Finally, unable even to try to eat the food, she stopped eating altogether.

To avoid the long hours with nothing to do, Benazir began keeping a daily diary in a small notebook. It had been secretly given to her by a sympathetic jail keeper. Carefully, she recorded events inside and outside the prison. Fortunately, some of her jailers could be trusted. They took the notes away every day and hid them safely. Benazir was also allowed to read one newspaper every day, which she read over and over again.

Each day, her captors warned her of a possible trial and death sentence. During the five months she spent in Sukkur Jail, Benazir continued to grow thinner. Worried that she might die in jail, the police shifted her back to the Karachi Central jail, where she hoped to see her mother. Instead, she was pushed into a dark, dirty cell. To her, surprise, she was taken to a hospital the next day. The guards said she had uterine cancer. She had known nothing about this, and had not given her consent for an operation.

At the hospital, Sanam, younger sister of Benazir Bhutto, was permitted to visit her for thirty minutes. She found Benazir drugged, screaming about her father's death, and fears of her own death.

Two days after her operation, Benazir was flown back to Sukkur Jail. Years later, Benazir heard that a former Pakistani minister in the PPP received a telephone call in London about the government's attempt to kill Benazir Bhutto on the operating table. The minister immediately gave a press conference and reported this information to the London newspapers. Benazir does not know for certain if her death was Zia's intent, but she feels sure the public attention helped save her life.

Meanwhile, the Pakistani newspapers were making terrible accusations against Mir and Shah for heading a secret organization called Al-Zulfikar from Afghanistan. The articles also claimed that Nusrat and Benazir knew about this. Benazir was angered, especially when she heard that Zia was arresting and torturing those who had any connection to the name of Bhutto.

Within her jail cell, Benazir was suffering from a different kind of torture,. The daytime heat in May soared to 120° F (48° C). The hot desert dust swirled into her cell crusting her face. Her skin cracked and peeled, and unsightly blisters appeared on her face. Without the proper diet, her hair began to fall out in clumps, too.

At this point, Benazir says, her jail officials began suggesting suicide as a way to end her physical suffering. They told her that her party leaders and followers were deserting her. "I prayed to Gad to give me strength," she said later. To her jailers, she said, "If I am the only person left resisting the tyranny of the regime, then so be it. I don't believe your lies."

In this weakened condition, Benazir celebrated her twenty-eighth birthday. Her sister Sanam was the only visitor. Sanam brought some happy news at last—she planned to marry Nasser Hussein, a longtime friend of their brothers. Benazir could not have been happier for her sister, feeling that this step would help protect her. Nasser had a successful telecommunications business, and Benazir thought he was a good person.

After Sanam had left, Benazir turned to prayer. Each day she hoped for a miracle. Then one day, the matron of the jail opened the gate to her cell and told Benazir she was leaving.

For a moment, Benazir was hopeful. Perhaps she would at last be allowed to return to her home in Karachi. There, she would see her mother, who had been sent home recently after having been found coughing up blood in her Karachi cell.

The police vehicles screeched out of Sukkur Jail, sped over the canal locks, and raced along the crumbling tarmac to Sukkur airport, where Benazir was placed on a plane to Karachi. There, she was met by army vehicles that passed the turn-off to her home, dashing her hopes for a family reunion.

3

Her Entry into Politics

Benazir Bhutto never planned to enter into politics. Her father was at the peak of his political career when he was deposed and hanged. The situation that followed thrust political choice on her. General Zia-ul-Haq made all possible efforts end the Bhutto family and Benazir and her mother Nusrat Bhutto were the first to face his fury.

The army convoy switched on their sirens to force their way through the traffic of Karachi until they drove into the familiar compound of dried, baked earth. Ahead was the Central jail, a sturdy looking fortress trimmed in blue. There, Benazir entered the first iron gate and climbed through a hole in the red and blue steel door into a dark hall. This led to the superintendent's office. From there, she squeezed through another hole into an open-walled compound. She was pushed through the final gate into a cell that had once held her own mother. The feeling, of depression on that August day in 1981 was almost more than she could bear.

Benazir's cell was inside a locked courtyard. All the prisoners had been moved out of the adjoining cells, leaving her alone except for a jail matron. The cell was smaller than the one at Sukkur jail. The walls were peeling, and the ceiling fan didn't work. Only the barred windows gave off limited light and air. Benazir could hardly breathe from the wet heat of the Karachi summer.

"Sometimes in jail," she recalls, "I would indulge in self-pity and say to myself, 'Why do I have to suffer so much?' Then, I would feel guilty and focus on God and be grateful. I used to cry in my pillow at night."

The dead silence at night was even more frightening than being locked in jail. After sunset, she thought she heard noises and voices, but her guards told her she was imagining the sounds. These words reminded her of her father's jail terms. People had walked on the roof of his cell, attempting to break his calm and make him think he was going mad. Once Benazir realized this, she began praying regularly, trying, to ignore all of the sounds. They eventually stopped.

Longing to see her mother, Benazir was finally allowed a short visit from her. She was shocked at Nusrat Bhutto's appearance. Benazir had remembered her mother as elegant and beautiful, not as this thin, old woman with gray hair. Because of the listening guards, the two women talked mostly about Nusrat's health. According to the doctors, she was suffering from either tuberculosis—a lung disease—or lung cancer.

After Nusrat left, Benazir felt even more lonely than she had before. She began to think about her family's misfortunes: she was in solitary confinement, her father was dead, her mother was ill, and her two brothers were somewhere in a distant land.

The only way to dismiss these thoughts of self-pity was to focus on events outside her world. She did this by reading newspapers. From them, she learned that the United States was now taking notice of Pakistan because of the Soviet invasion into Afghanistan. Before this, the U.S. government had withdrawn aid from Pakistan for fear it was developing its own nuclear bomb.

When Ronald Reagan defeated jimmy Carter in the 1980 presidential elections, the U.S. government began providing money to Pakistan again. In order to prevent the Soviet forces from pushing over the borders into Pakistan, the United States supplied General Zia with millions of dollars and supplies. Reportedly, Zia kept large amounts of this aid for himself. He told the world that Pakistan was fighting communism. A spokesperson for the American State Department called him a "world statesman" and a "benevolent [kindly] dictator." Further aid came from international food organizations to help support the Afghan refugees entering Pakistan.

As Benazir sat in her cell and read about Zia becoming a hero in the eyes of the Western world, she was torn between discouragement and anger. Unable to think about the political situation in Pakistan without becoming enraged, Benazir tried to concentrate on her sister's wedding. It would be held in Karachi on September 8, 1981. The jail superintendent offered to free her for the wedding if she would give up politics completely. Benazir refused.

On the evening of the wedding, the prison matron came to Benazir suddenly and told her she had permission to go to Sanam's wedding. In a daze, Benazir was taken in a train of police cars to 70 Clifton. As she stepped into the courtyard at the front entrance, she was greeted with the scent of jasmine and roses, and the sounds of festive music. Her relatives, who had come from as far as California, England, France, and all parts of Pakistan, rushed to embrace her.

Benazir's first step was to take a hot bath. As she tried to wash away the grime from weeks in her unsanitary cell, she began to put aside the hardships of jail. Sipping the pure, cold water was another luxury she had missed.

Benazir spent the next two days reading international and national publications, and talking with her mother and sister. Benazir was happy that Sanam'sAssassination of Benazir Bhutto was not an arranged marriage, as was typical in Pakistan. Nasser Hussein had risked the displeasure of his family in marrying Sanam. They considered the Bhutto name a dangerous one. Nasser and Sanam had stood up for themselves, though, and Benazir was very glad for them.

As part of the traditional wedding ceremony, the reddish brown henna dye, called *mehndi*, was used to paint beautiful scrolls and pictures on the hands and feet of the ladies. Under a canopy, the wedding couple sat on cushions inlaid with tiny sparkling mirrors. The guests chanted songs about the conditions of the marriage, and what each partner would do for the other.

The police interrupted the ceremonies several times, serving notices to Nusrat and, in general, trying to upset the Bhutto family. Benazir had become so used to their methods and to her life in prison that she caught herself referring to the jail as her home.

Ignoring the police disturbances, the wedding continued. The bride and groom were each asked three times if they agreed to the marriage. At the end of the marriage vows, the couple looked into a mirror placed between them to recognize their new married state. Watching them, Benazir felt her eyes fill with tears.

When the ceremony was over, Benazir hastily wrote a letter to Peter Galbraith, her friend from Harvard and Oxford. She had learned during the wedding that he had come to Pakistan, demanding to see her in jail. He had carried with him a letter from the Senate Foreign Relations Committee which also asked that he be allowed to see her. He was turned down, but had returned to the United States determined to help the Bhutto women.

Benazir's letter to Peter Galbraith said, among other things, "Did they teach us that life could be full of such terrible dangers and tragedies.... Freedom and liberty, the essays we wrote on them, papers for our tutors, for grades, but did we know the value of those words which we bandied about, or how precious they are, as precious as the air we breathe, the water we drink."

Finally, the wedding celebration was over, and Benazir was taken back to jail. This time, she was taken to a smaller, darker cell. There, she would read, write, and think about her country and its future.

On December 11, 1981, the deputy superintendent came to Benazir's cell and told her to pack her belongings. She would be taken to Larkana the next morning under police escort. Strangely enough, Benazir was sad to leave the Karachi Central Jail. At least she knew what to expect there.

The next day, she was driven to her family home, AlMurtaza. She was told she would be free to use the telephone and have visitors. Her happiness at this news did not last long. The only visitors she could have were a few relatives. She was allowed no telephone calls, except to and from relatives. She tried to learn how to cook to make the long, dull days pass quickly.

Along with these difficulties came news that Nusrat Bhutto's health was not good. In fact, news that she had cancer had been leaked to reporters in London and other cities. This resulted in another campaign to "save the Bhutto ladies." Zia, however, did not want Nusrat to leave Pakistan. He directed her doctor to sign a report claiming that further medical treatment was not necessary. Risking his personal safety, Nusrat's physician refused to follow Zia's orders, as did all the doctors on the medical board.

On November 20, 1982, Nusrat was allowed to travel to West Germany and Switzerland for medical treatment. To say farewell to her mother, Benazir was driven under heavy military guard to the airport, and flown to Karachi after eleven months in Larkana.

Feeling lonely, Benazir parted from her mother at 70 Clifton. Instead of returning to Larkana, Benazir was placed under house arrest in Karachi for another fourteen months.

In December 1982, General Zia made an official visit to the United States to meet with President Ronald Reagan. There, the Senate Foreign Relations Committee challenged him with the reported abuse of political prisoners in Pakistan. When they demanded to know the location of Benazir Bhutto, he lost his temper and said, "I can tell you she lives in a better house than any senator and is allowed visitors and can use the telephone."

To challenge that statement, Peter Galbraith telephoned the Bhutto residence in Karachi and asked to speak to Benazir. "You cannot speak to her. It is forbidden," was the answer. Even after identifying himself and saying he had President Zia's permission, the guards refused to let him speak to her.

Unaware of these efforts, Benazir began 1983 ill and tense. She began grinding her teeth at night, and woke to find her knuckles swollen. The problems with her ear returned, too, and would not go away. To try to ease the pain and isolation, she prayed daily to God.

Meanwhile, the Senate Foreign Relations Committee, under the constant pressure of Peter Galbraith, kept asking Pakistan about Benazir Bhutto's confinement, The committee personally asked Pakistan's foreign minister on his Washington visit about Bhutto's treatment. He was shocked by the facts they presented to him, and promised to investigate immediately.

Despite her physical problems, Benazir was encouraged by news that the Movement to Restore Democracy (MRD) was still resisting the military. Taking heart from this news, Benazir wrote encouraging letters to the group with her mother's name on them. She did not want to use her own name for fear she would be punished for taking part in illegal activities. She thought that her mother, now living in Europe, would be safe from any punishment.

By June 1983, the infection in Benazir's ear was constant. Her doctor told the authorities that Benazir needed special treatment in Europe. In December, the government granted her permission to go to Switzerland for surgery. When they gave her the news, Benazir could hardly believe it. She was afraid to show any emotion or excitement. Her feelings, after seven years, had become numb.

Politics in Exile

In January 1984, Benazir Bhutto stepped from the airplane onto the runway in Geneva, Switzerland. Her eyes, used to darkness from her years in prison, squinted in the blinding sunlight. Her mother was there to greet her and Sanam. "Yesterday, I was a prisoner. Today, I am free with my mother and sister. We are together. We are all alive," Benazir said gratefully.

The reunion was a very happy one, interrupted by telephone calls from relatives and well-wishers. Benazir's brother Mir, who was living in Switzerland, came to see her with his little daughter, eighteen-month-old Fathi. Mir, now twenty-nine, was handsome and gentle. Her other brother, Shah, could not come from the south of France to meet her. The last time she had seen him, he had been eighteen years old. He was now twenty-five.

As much as Benazir wanted to stay close to her reunited family, she needed to go to London for medical treatment. She also wanted to continue her political opposition to Zia. This she could do in England. At that time, there were already 378,000 Pakistanis living in the country.

Sanam, who now lived in London with her husband, travelled with Benazir to London's Heathrow Airport. Word had spread among the Pakistani community of her arrival, and a large crowd awaited her. Strangers thought Benazir was a movie star. When they learned she was a political leader, they asked if she was going into exile.

"I was born in Pakistan and I'm going to die in Pakistan," she replied. To her fellow Pakistanis, she said, "I am not giving up on you. I will stay by your side until my last breath. The Bhuttos keep their promises."

For a short while, Benazir was a guest at her Aunt Behjat's apartment in London's Knightsbridge section. The telephone never stopped ringing, and visitors streamed through the apartment at all hours. But when a car, filled with Pakistani men, began following Benazir wherever she went, she became suspicious. Her aunt called Scotland Yard, the detective department of the London police. The car soon vanished from in front of the apartment building.

Benazir had difficulties adjusting to her freedom. A fear of crowds, and of being followed, bothered her. Even the closed-in feeling of the underground subway kept her above ground, using taxis for all her travel. Not wanting to disappoint the Pakistanis who looked to her as a strong figure, she kept these fears to herself.

Shortly after her arrival in London, Peter Galbraith arrived and met with Benazir. He had flown to Pakistan to try to see her, but found out she had already been released. He had not seen her since 1977, and noticed that she had a new self-confidence. They discussed the personal changes in their lives and those of their friends.

Peter tried to persuade Benazir to go to America and apply for a fellowship at Harvard. "My first obligation is to the party. In political terms, it makes more sense for me to be here, where the Pakistani community is larger," she replied.

Finally, in late January, Benazir underwent surgery on her ear. The doctors told her it would take nine months for her to recover. Nusrat Bhutto's health had greatly improved since she left Pakistan. She now came from Switzerland and rented an apartment in the London suburbs where she could help restore her daughter's health.

During these long months, Benazir developed a plan to wage a publicity campaign in the international press. She wanted to expose the cruel treatment of 40,000 political prisoners held in Pakistan. She began by providing specific information to Amnesty International, a worldwide organization that seeks to have political prisoners freed.

As a result of these efforts, the Carnegie Endowment for International Peace in Washington, D.C., invited Bhutto to speak in March 1984. With her girlhood friend Yasmin Niazi, she flew to the United States to speak for the Carnegie Endowment. She also visited senators and State Department officials. She asked for their public support in demanding the release of political prisoners in Pakistan.

In the Senate Foreign Relations Committee, they asked her if aid to Pakistan should be stopped. As much as Bhutto was opposed to Zia's policies, she answered by saying, "Cutting off aid will only create misunderstandings between the two countries. Both our countries would be better served if aid were linked to the restoration of human rights and democracy to Pakistan." The committee decided to continue aid to Pakistan.

Upon returning to England, Bhutto found an apartment to rent near Saint Paul's Cathedral. It had security guards, which reduced her fear of unwanted visitors, and let her check the people coming and going. The small apartment became the headquarters for the Pakistan People's Party (PPP) abroad.

Once again, Bhutto increased her efforts to save her country's political prisoners. Her first effort was to produce a news magazine in both Urdu and English. Benazir also travelled all over England and other parts of Europe, speaking to Pakistani groups. She slowly established a small, but growing, opposition to Zia.

Faced with this threat, Zia sentenced many prisoners to death. Benazir protested these executions by appealing to Elliot Abrams, the Assistant Secretary of State for Human Rights. She also spoke to members of Parliament.

United States government leaders, too, began to put pressure on Zia. They insisted he hold general elections in Pakistan, which he agreed to schedule for March 1985. But first, he announced a referendum for December 20, 1984. This would give the people of Pakistan an opportunity to say whether or not they wanted elections to be held. Zia told the Pakistanis that a vote for general elections would be a vote against Islam.

Through their news magazine and a secret organization in Pakistan and abroad, Benazir Bhutto and the PPP attempted to inform voters about the referendum. They urged people to boycott the vote. The Manchester Guardian, a London newspaper, later reported that only 10 per cent of Pakistanis had voted. The government, however, clamed 64 per cent had voted.

After the referendum, general elections were scheduled for March. PPP leaders suggested that Benazir Bhutto return to Pakistan to challenge Zia. The suggestion was soon dismissed when Benazir learned that her Karachi home was surrounded by the army. A warrant for the arrest of Nusrat and Benazir had been issued.

The March election was held, and Zia won-although the turnout was again very low. Zia then announced that he would change his government from a military to a civilian government.

Sadly, the execution of political prisoners continued. Frustrated, Benazir Bhutto spoke out publicly. She spoke at Harvard in 1985, addressing the Council on Foreign Relations. She also delivered a speech to the members of the European Parliament in Strasbourg.

At Strasbourg, she said, "When the conscience of the world is justly aroused against apartheid and against human rights violations... then that conscience ought not to close its eyes to the murder by military courts which takes place in a country which receives... aid from the West itself." Following this speech, more than 54 prisoners in Lahore were sentenced to death.

In mid-1985, Benazir felt she needed a break from the constant pressures of politics. She arranged a vacation with members of her family in the south of France.

After her plane landed in Cannes, Benazir looked around for someone to meet her. There was no one. Suddenly, her brother Shah jumped out from behind a pillar to surprise her. The other family members came out from their hiding places, too. Benazir was very happy to see her youngest brother.

Shah had always had a special fondness for Benazir. tie had written to her frequently when she had first left home to Harvard. Later, Ali Bhutto had sent Shah away to military school. He thought his mischievous young son needed to learn some discipline. For Shah, it was a very unhappy experience. He had pleaded with his mother to let him return to Islamabad and attend the International School there. She had finally agreed. Not only did Shah like to play pranks, he was very generous. If someone asked him for his coat, he would give, it away to them.

After Mir and Shah had escaped to Afghanistan at the time of the coup, they met and married sisters. Mir and Fauzia had eventually moved to Switzerland. Shah and his wife, Rehana, had a daughter named Sassi and were now living in Cannes, Unfortunately, Shah's marriage was not a happy one, and the couple only stayed together for the sake of their daughter.

Knowing this, Benazir was not surprised when Shah told her he intended to divorce his wife. Nevertheless, Benazir pleaded with him to make every effort to remain together. She also tried to befriend Rehana during her monthlong stay in Cannes, but found the other woman to be somewhat unfriendly.

On the morning Shah had planned to take Benazir to Nice, in southern France, the two Bhutto women received a disturbing phone call from Rehana. Something was wrong with Shah, she told them. He had taken poison.

What followed seemed a nightmare to Benazir. When she and Nusrat arrived at Shah's apartment, they found him dead on the living room floor. Although the official explanation was suicide, many people suspected a political murder.

Against the advice of friends and relatives, Benazir decided in August 1985 to take the body of her brother back to the family grave in Larkana, Pakistan. The Pakistani military leaders were not pleased with this decision, yet they could not stop the burial. Worldwide publicity and pressure would be bad for the current government.

The mourners crowded into Larkana and Karachi. Once again, the government detained Benazir. But this time, the U.S. State Department protested. In an official statement, a spokesperson said, "Pakistan has taken encouraging steps toward.., constitutional government.... Putting Ms. Bhutto under house arrest would appear... inconsistent with this process."

Meanwhile, Rehana had been arrested in connection with Shah's death, and Benazir had been asked to appear in court. In November, she was allowed to leave Pakistan to testify in Nice, France. Due to the suspicions against Rehana, Mir and Fauzia had separated.

Eventually, Sassi, Shah's daughter, was sent to live with grandparents in the United States. To this day, the Bhuttos do not know where she is. They refuse to give up hope, though, because Sassi's name means, "one who crosses the deserts and mountains to find the family who loves her."

"Difficulty is a part of everyday life," says Benazir Bhutto when remembering this period of her life. "I took my father for granted and lost him. My brother was so young when he died-and in a safe place like France. Suddenly, when those who are closest to you are gone, you think of all those unspoken words. We don't appreciate our mothers and fathers, and the gift they are to you."

Role of Benazir and Musharraf

Then came Pakistan's ten-year-long honeymoon with democracy under Benazir Bhutto and Nawaz Sharif. As they replaced each other twice over, some policies changed. But one thing remained unchanged: the government's hobnobbing with extremists and fundamentalists. Benazir legitimised the fanatics of the JUI by bringing them into her government as a coalition partner and by appointing their firebrand leader, Fazlur, Rahman, as chairman of a parliamentary committee. Her government, in close collaboration with the JUI, created the and put them in power in Afghanistan. The Taliban's emergence and its control over Afghanistan was regarded as a momentous victory for Pakistani strategists who had for long for "strategic depth". History is a witness to the fact that it was Benazir, a western-educated woman Prime Minister, who set in motion the events leading to 9/11.

For his part, Nawaz Sharif continued to appease the mullahs and the military and ironically for him the very military he sought to keep in good homour, overthrew him in a bloodless coup on October 12, 1999.

What the Pakistani rulers did, and are still doing, is that they struck at the very root of the country's development: the educational system. It would not be an exaggeration to say that no other area of Pakistani society has been penetrated by radical Islam to a greater extent than the educational system. Today, Pakistan's huge network of Islamic seminaries, in every region of the country, churns out hundreds of thousands of fanatics year after year. This is in sharp contrast to India which produces the largest number of engineering and medical graduates every year in the world.

It would be simplistic to believe that President Pervez Musharraf is unaware of the existence of jihadi madrasas and terrorist groups in Pakistan. It would be equally fallacious to assess that he has failed in controlling them. The truth is he has allowed jihadi madrasas and terrorist groups to prosper despite the international pressure.

Even the Pakistan press has said it openly. *The Daily Times*, a widely respected English daily published from Lahore, said the "the government appeared to resume a task it had abandoned earlier in the year. It sent inspection teams into the seminaries and mosques all over the country and arrested nearly a hundred people charged with possessing and disseminating hate literature." This, the newspaper said, implied that President Musharraf's government had given up the job which, he had claimed more than twice as an important objective in national interest.

The speed and the extent of the present police crackdown also reveals another fact–the authorities were aware of the activities of these jihadi groups but were neither interested nor authorised to take action. In Islamabad, alone, for instance, the security agencies rounded up more than 40 people, including Mufti Ibrar, personal secretary to the leader of the opposition in the National Assembly, Maulana Fazlur Rehman. Eight seminaries were raided in the city, including Madrasa Jamia al-Hafsa, commonly known as Lal Masjid, which is said to be the most powerful stronghold of the Deobandis. Shia madrasas also raided as part of the crackdown.

It is significant to note that the Pakistan authorities had a shut eye when suicide bombers from the same set of seminaries attacked Islamabad's Barri Imam shrine. Similarly, when a feeble attempt to rein in these seminaries was made by the government in the wake of rising sectarian clashes, especially on the extremists owing allegiance to Lal Masjid and other seminaries in the neighbourhood politicians like Imran Khan had intervened and prevented the operation. The imam of Lal Masjid had escaped a number of sectarian attacks from the rival sectarian party,

The sweep and depth of the raids in Punjab, Khushab, Faisalabad, DG Khan and Multan, all known Deobandi and Ahle Hadith centres of power, also betrayed the number and strength of jihadi madrasas in Pakistan. *The Daily Times* said in the last few years, donations from local philanthropists in the country amounted to about Rs. 140 billion annually, of which some Rs. 90 billion was in cash. About 80 per cent of this amount was received by religious organisations for running mosques, madrasas, orphanages and other such facilities.

Besides deliberate laxity, there is another reason why President Musharraf has been ignoring the existence of terrorist groups and jihadi madrasas. Groups like Lashkar are critical to Pakistan's continuing proxy war against India. Without groups like Lashkar and Hijbul Mujahideen, Pakistan's claims on Kashmir will come to a naught.

Lashkar-e-Toiba is the terrorist group mainly responsible for killings in Kashmir. It is not that the General is merely tolerating some sort of fringe elements; he is deeply involved with them, with their agenda. Before coming to India to talk peace both in Agra (2001) and New Delhi (2005), President Musharraf had made it a point to consult the jihadi leaders.

There is another pointer to President Musharraf's deliberate indifference to the functioning of terrorist groups. The jihadi literature is freely available throughout Pakistan. Though President Musharraf on July 16, 2005, addressing senior police officials, ordered the confiscation of pamphlets, booklets and compact discs (CDs) promoting jihad, extremism, sectarian hatred in the wake of the July 7, 2005 London blasts, the hate literature is being openly sold in markets like Mohala Jhangi in Peshawar. Mohala Jhang market is the hub of Islamic literature and audio and video cassettes on jihad and Islam. The audio cassettes that are sold here contain speeches of militant leaders glorifying jihad against 'infidels' and CDs featuring leaders like Maulana Fazlur Rehman and Qazi Hussain Ahmed speaking on the need to implement Islamic system in the country. Speeches of leaders of banned sectarian organisations like Maulana Azam Tariq are also available in the market. Also available are video cassettes and CDs of footage of Afghan and Kashmir jihad, Iraq war, including execution of kidnapped foreigners in Iraq, and military operations against militants in South Waziristan.

There is no official nation-wide study of these madrasas. Estimates of their overall number range between 10,000 and 50,000. As for the number of students, here the estimate ranges from a conservative half-million to over 2 million, the latter figure being at par with the number of Pakistani children who attend primary schools.

Why the madrasas are so popular despite their extremist outlook and despite the fact that every analyst and strategic affairs writer has commented on these schools of terror. One does not have to go far to seek an answer to this question. The madrasas are the only source for an average Pakistani to put his or her ward in "school" which takes care of the ward's boarding and lodging free of cost. In a country that spends only $8 per capita on education, in a country where sixty per cent of the children are denied a chance to enroll in primary school, the madrasas are the only fight the average Pakistani sees at the end of the tunnel.

There are no official figures of the total expenditure incurred by the madrasas in Pakistan. A recent study by a Peshawar thinktank puts the cost of food alone in schools in the North West Frontier Province at $129 million per year, while total running costs for the madrasas in Pakistan are said by another source to be significantly higher than the "federal government's budgetary allocation for education, health, family planning, etc." The sum total is almost certainly well in excess of $1 billion a year.

It is a peculiar situation wherein the clerics themselves refuse to divulge the sources or the magnitude of the funding they receive for madrasas, the government has no means of obtaining such information because the madrasas are exempt from normal auditing procedures. One fact remains: domestic funding of the madrasas seldom exceeds 25 per cent of the total funds, which means that three-quarters of madrasa funding comes from abroad.

4

Her Policies

Introduction

Bhutto herself was also arrested many times. She was detained for three years before being permitted to leave the country in 1984. She settled in London, but along with her two brothers, she founded an underground organization to resist the military dictatorship. When her brother died in 1985, she returned to Pakistan for his burial, and was again arrested for participating in anti-government rallies.

She returned to London after her release, and martial law was lifted in Pakistan at the end of the year. Anti-Zia demonstrations resumed and Benazir Bhutto returned to Pakistan in April 1986. The public response to her return was tumultuous, and she publicly called for the resignation of Zia ul Haq.

She was elected co-chairperson of the Pakistan People's Party (PPP) along with her mother, and when free elections were finally held in 1988, she herself became Prime Minister. At 35, she was one of the youngest chief executives in the world, and the first woman to serve as prime minister in an Islamic country.

Only two years into her first term, President Ghulam Ishaq Khan dismissed Bhutto from office. She initiated an anti-corruption campaign, and in 1993 was re-elected as Prime Minister. While in office, she brought electricity to the countryside and built schools all over the country. She made hunger, housing and health care her top priorities, and looked forward to continuing to modernize Pakistan.

At the same time, Bhutto faced constant opposition from the Islamic fundamentalist movement. Her brother Mir Murtaza, who had been estranged from Benazir since their father's death, returned from abroad and levelled charges of corruption against Benazir's husband, Asif Ali Zardari. Mir Murtaza died when his bodyguard became involved in a gunfight with police in Karachi. The Pakistani public was shocked by this turn of events and PPP supporters were divided over the charges against Zardari.

In 1996, President Leghari dismissed Benazir Bhutto from office, alleging mismanagement, and dissolved the National Assembly. A Bhutto re-election bid failed in 1997, and the next elected government, headed by the more conservative Nawaz Sharif, was overthrown by the military. Bhutto's husband was imprisoned, and once again, she was forced to leave her homeland. For nine years, she and her children lived in exile in London, where she continued to advocate the restoration of democracy in Pakistan. In the autumn of 2007, in the face of death threats from radical Islamists, and the hostility of the government, she returned to her native country.

Economy

The PPP government presided over boom economies during its three tenures in office. Sound macro-economic management allows private entrepreneurs to build investment, trade and develop the economy. The PPP tripled growth rates and doubled the national revenues while enjoying lowest deficit figures and bringing in massive investment which created jobs and promoted the service industry including housing.

Free Flow of Capital

As the party that introduced the privatisation bill and streamlined the revenue services while creating boards at local bank branches for quick disbursement of loans, the PPP is committed to the free flow of capital. The flow of capital is the engine that drives a growing economy encouraging the youth while ending unemployment which brings misery.

Introduction of an Autonomous State Bank

PPP introduced an autonomous State Bank and a strong regulatory authority, necessary to safeguard the deposits of the working and middle classes in the banking sector. The seizure of foreign exchange reserves and collapse of cooperatives as well as investment companies when PPP was in opposition robbed ordinary citizens.

PPP Power Projects

PPP power projects, mass telephone system enabled ordinary people to set up businesses when previously power shutdowns and twenty year waiting lines for phone prevented them from success in private initiatives. PPP focuses on making the changes that help people make successful businesses. PPP times are boom times for the business communities as well as for the labour that is absorbed by a booming market.

Adoption of the Pay as You Earn Scheme

To support middle class purchases, the Pay As You Earn Scheme (Credit Purchases) was adopted in Government Corporations and other salaried institutions. A credit bank was established, the purpose of which would be small and medium loans to encourage installment purchases of television, furniture, cars, houses, refrigerators and other household and daily life necessities which are too expensive for outright purchase by young and middle age purchasers.

This scheme will be expanded to include non-salaried institutions gradually.

Open Minds, Open Markets, Open opportunities is PPP's slogan.

The party believes that a democratic government is necessary for sound macro management as well as for investment, revenues, growth, employment and safeguarding the savings of the people.

Education

Quaid e Awam Zulfikar Ali Bhutto, believed that education was the key to the empowerment of the people. He introduced free and compulsory primary education, promoted centres of excellence, created Institutes of Science and Technology and took Pakistan to the cutting edge of nuclear physics establishing centres of nuclear medicine. He set up a chain of new universities, medical and engineering colleges in the neglected areas as a harbinger to a Muslim renaissance. Western countries developed by encouraging free debate in universities of excellence which produce the men and women needed to govern great nations.

Enhancement of Computer Literacy Programme

Textbooks to government primary schools will be provided free of cost while a means test will make students eligible for additional government support. Libraries will be promoted and vocational centres, on the pattern of the Computer Literacy Programme, enhanced.

Access to the Internet

Internet access for government schools will enable the children of the underprivileged to access the worldwide information highway. The global language, English, will be an optional language for students to study preventing lingual apartheid where children of the rich speak English competing for world wide jobs and children of the working classes are denied that opportunity.

Increase in Education Budget

Seeking an age of reason and enlightenment, the PPP, which increased with extra billions education budget in its two recent terms of power, pledges to make education a top priority. It is education, and education alone that can enable our young people to realise their full potential and compete with the best that the world can produce in the field of art and science. PPP Parliamentarians commit to its sons and daughters an education that enables a brighter future than that of their parents so that they can hold high their head sin the comity of nations.

Human Rights

The plight of women, minorities, children and the wretched of the earth is miserable. It is a deep stigma on our national conscience that disadvantaged groups suffered a series of punishments, laws, public humiliations and gang rapes while the state watched helplessly. The PPP is committed to promote and protect human rights.

Protection of the Weak from the Strong

The PPP Parliamentarians pledge to protect the minorities, women and children of Pakistan . It pledges to protect the weak from the strong. It pledges to undo laws that are discriminatory against minorities, women and children. It calls upon the people of Pakistan to give it a constitutional majority to build a society where the weak and underprivileged are freed from archaic state laws.

Women and Children

The PPP Parliamentarians pledge to promote universal female literacy and protection of the child to honour thewomen and the future generations.

Encouragement to NGOs

The PPP Parliamentarians will encourage non-governmental organisations as watchdogs for the empowerment of women and minorities.

Poverty

The overthrow of the PPP government in 1996 led to the impoverishment of the people of Pakistan. For the first time in recorded history, mass unemployment reached such heights that people chose to commit suicide because they were unable to feed their families.

A country which under the PPP became one of the ten emerging capital markets of the world, attracting massive foreign investment became a barren landscape. Investors fled from the country as they were unjustly scandalised in politically motivated allegations by hostile regimes seeking to score political points.

The bill was picked up by the unfortunate people of the country whose per capita income fell as the gap between the rich and the poor widened. The PPP had revenues to build schools, hospitals, roads and provide people with basic amenities. The regimes that replaced it froze foreign accounts, raised utility bills, retrenched hundred of thousands of employees without any benefit to the country. They brazenly cut the budgets that the PPP so painstakingly built for important programmes including education, health, women's empowerment, youth, population control, labour and the rural poor. They did this even as they hired favourites at exorbitant salaries paid in advance.

The PPP Parliamentarians pledge to eradicate poverty by ensuring that the social sector budget is increased as is the Annual Development Plan. It is by investing in young people that can build a progressive and prosperous society.

Labour

Created as the party to protect labour rights, the PPP introduced the reform for minimum wages, cost of living, social security, medical cover, old age benefits, pensions and other such measures for the betterment of the working classes.

Protection of Labour Rights

The PPP is proud of its record where labour rights were fully protected. PPP Parliamentarians oppose retrenchment of labour. It pledges to hold high the banner of labour rights with a view to ensuring that labour enjoy a good working relationship with the government while enhancing productivity.

Supporting Laws in Accordance with the ILO

PPP is opposed to contract labour as well as retrenchment of labour. It supports wage increases for labour, given the high rates of inflation. It supports laws in accordance with the International Labour Organisation.

Establishment of Labour Welfare Funds

PPP will review the situation with a view to providing relief to retrenched workers. Additionally, it will use labour welfare funds to build residential colonies for workers. Establish cadet colleges for children of labour force.

Defence

The PPP gave Pakistan a strong defence to safeguard its territorial integrity and national independence. The Quaid-e-Awam gave Pakistan the nuclear programme to achieve nuclear parity with India. Mohtarma Benazir Bhutto gave Pakistan missile capability to enable the country to match the Indian missile threat.

The PPP believes that a sound economic base promotes a strong defence. It seeks to identify Pakistan's core defence needs to enable the country to meet its defence targets.

Inspection of Defence Accounts

The PPP opposes waste and extravagance through non-audited accounts and re-appropriation of budgets. It plans putting in place a parliamentary committee to inspect defence accounts which will also be submitted to the defence committee of the cabinet.

Transparency in Defence Purchases

Concerned about corruption in defence deals, the PPP plans greater transparency in defence purchases and a rationalisation of defence expenditure to make the armed forces fit and professional as they were before the military dictatorship of General Zia in discharging their core responsibility of defending the territorial integrity and frontiers of Pakistan.

Revision of Educational Curriculum in Defence Institutes

The educational curriculum in defence institutes was prepared to train an officer cadre that could uphold the forces of military rule. That curriculum will be revised to ensure military respect for democracy, democratic institutions and elected officials. The true face of military dictatorship will be open in courses to encourage officers to prevent the past with a view to building a better future in accordance with the principles of Quaid e Azam.

Judicial Relief

Easy dispensation of justice is the right of citizens. Too many suffer because of their inability to access justice.

Appointment of Judicial Ombudsmen

Innocent people languish in jails without the funds to obtain judicial relief. Each High Court will appoint Judicial Ombudsman to visit jails and police stations providing relief to those deserving it.

Increase in Number of Courts

Number of courts will be increased as well as number of judges to ensure that cases are dealt with expeditiously.

Special courts will be abolished.

Examination of Law of Foreclosure

Law of foreclosure will be examined in discussion with the judiciary. It is strong foreclosures in developed countries that enable the middle classes to obtain credit for purchases such as apartments, cars, televisions and similar products where lenders know that defaulters can be taken to task without a stay order.

Fair and Easy Justice

Small Causes Courts and Family Court at the local bodies' level can assist fair and easy justice.

More women and minority judges will be inducted into the judiciary.

Health

Won the World Health Organisation Gold medal

Having eliminated polio, iodised salt and inoculated children in deadly diseases, the PPP pledges investment in health. Its previous health policies won it the World Health Organisation Gold medal.

Increase in Health Expenditures

It increased health expenditures in the past seeing in a healthy body a healthy society. Elimination of lead poisoning and other simple measures can improve the quality of health with small initiatives quantifying into big results.

Assistance to Homeless People

PPP will improve government health centres and hospitals. It will establish Old Peoples Homes as well as Homes for Poor Children to aid and assist families that find such issues challenging.

Debt

PPP is proud to have given Pakistan stability and the writ of the state in all its governments making the safety of citizens its top priority. It can do so again.

PPP Retired Capital Debt

The PPP was honoured to retire one billion dollars of Pakistan's mountain of debt that crushes its people and makes it a dependent nation. It's the only government that ever retired capital debt.

Regimes squandered opportunities that arose where Pakistan, like Egypt and Jordan, could have got the debt written off.

Strengthened the Economy

The PPP always took power after rulers signed agreements with international financial institutions locking it into pre fixed frameworks. As soon as the PPP strengthened the economy enabling it to negotiate a better deal with the international financial institutions, it was overthrown by the anti people forces.

Liberate from Poverty, Debt and Servitude

PPP will continue its reform process to liberate the people of Pakistan from the shackles of poverty, debt and servitude.

Internet

The PPP heralded the information age into Pakistan with colour television, fax machines, e-mails and satellite television. It laid optic fibre lines in 1989 to promote internet connections and digitalise telecommunications. In 1993, it began computer literacy programmes to herald the computer literate generation.

Promotion of Information Technology

PPP software parks in Islamabad, Karachi and Lahore will be revised. The state will actively equip the citizens to meet the demands of the future. It will give incentives for software development as well as hardware development. A special credit facility will be available for outstanding students to develop ideas in the field of artificial intelligence and the computer age. The government will supplement ordinary libraries with computer libraries and internet access.

Constitutional Package

To fulfil Quaid-e-Azam and Quaid-e-Awam's dream of a federal and democratic Pakistan where the provinces enjoy full autonomy, the Concurrent List will be abolished in keeping with the Constitutional commitments.

Examination of the Establishment of a Constitutional Court

The establishment of a Constitutional Court will be examined in consultation with the Pakistan Human Rights Commission as well as other bodies.

Tenures of District Councils

Tenures of District Councils will be fixed and free from interference other than through the judicial process to establish a pluralistic society where different parties can exercise power at different levels. Simultaneously, preventing a culture of exclusion and winner takes all. This can enhance tolerance and accommodation within the body politic of the country.

Constitutional Protection of Election Commission

Election Commission will be constitutionally protected although its actions can be scrutinised through appeal to high courts. Election Tribunal cases must be decided expeditiously.

Police Reform

Independence of the Police System

The independence of the police system will be encouraged enabling the force to groom a professional body which is tough on crime and criminals. The unfortunate history of political taint which demoralises the police force and oppreses the citizens will be done away with. Police will be treated on par with military officers and entitled to similar benefits. A strong and professional police force is necessary to combat the forces of internal terrorism.

Prohibition of Use of Torture

Use of torture will be prohibited and police training institutes upgraded with modern means of forensic evidence and interrogation.

Recruitment of Police Force

Local recruitment of the police force will be encouraged with matriculation as a minimum qualification.

Examination of Allegation of Torture and Corruption

Allegations of torture and corruption will be examined by a Police Ombudsman appointed by the Inspector General of Police.

Prison Reforms

PPP aims at reforming prisoners enabling them to integrate into society as responsible citizens. Concept of hard labour is outdated and can be abolished. Prisoners will be encouraged to take classes to learn skills and earn points towards good behaviour early release. They will be paid proper wages for work undertaken and be entitled to purchase facilities for themselves including television, computers and other products. Communal rooms will provide internet access to selected sites as well as reading material in libraries which is commensurate with modern publications. Exercise classes will be held separately for men and women prisoners for those wishing to avail of it. Medical attention will be given promptly. Proper seating arrangements for interviews will be made.

Prisoners will have the right to make available transport for going to court hearings in the event of vehicle shortage.

Prison Administration

Presently, prison administration is a prisoner of the home secretary. Prison administration will be given rules within which to function and will be autonomous in its functioning. Complaints by government or prisoners can be made to the Home Secretary and officers which will be reviewable before the judicial authorities. Postings to prisons will be by tenure and officials transferred earlier only on the basis of written complaints which can form basis of a discrimination appeal.

Housing of Female Prisoners

Female prisoners will be housed in separate quarters and looked after by female staff. No male staff will be permitted entrance to the female quarters. Female quarters will have similar facilities as male quarters with additional child care areas.

Farmers

The vast majority of the people of the country are farmers eking out an existence in challenging circumstances where water is in shortage.

It is the job of government to ensure that the farmers get a good deal for their hard work.

A Farmer Friendly Policy

The PPP government ensured a farmer friendly policy which gave the country high growth rates and productivity with yields going up from zero per cent to seven per cent. The Awami tractor scheme providing tractors at one and a half lakhs was part of the initiative that helped farmers.

The PPP pledges to look after the farmer with timely inputs of fertilisers, seeds and water. It promises to give the farmer his due where prices are concerned and relieve him from poverty through appropriate access to credit.

Water Logging and Salinity

The threat of water logging and salinity will be countered with greater resource commitment by the government and the completion of canals to serve that purpose. Small hydel dams begun under the last government will continue.

Drinking and Agricultural Water

Shortage of drinking and agricultural water is the greatest challenge in the twenty first century which will be met through the close cooperation between government, farmers and technical experts.

Peace

Birth of Violence

The oppressors of the people used religious parties as well as the strategic location of Pakistan to exploit international opinion in a bid to gain legitimacy. Their politics gave birth to violence and the Kalashnikov culture.

Military Dictators and Afghanistan

An earlier military dictator used Afghanistan's critical importance to the world community to perpetuate his own dictatorship. Now another military dictator is attempting to use Afghanistan to perpetuate himself at the cost of the fundamental and human rights, including economic rights, of the people of the country.

Concentration of Absolute Power

The concentration of absolute power is detrimental to the welfare and prosperity of the country. It threatens to give birth to ethnicity, poverty and violence. It threatens to make Pakistan another Yugoslavia. Every patriotic citizen must rise up to save Pakistan from an unfortunate fate.

Pakistan Must Seek Peace Within and Peace Without

The former Soviet Union collapsed under the weight of its military dominance. Other countries collapsed under the weight of civil war leading to massive bloodshed played out on international television screens. To save Pakistan from such a calamity towards which the absolute concentration of power threatens to lead the nation, the word of Muhammad Ali Jinnah are worth quoting.

He said, "Pakistan must seek peace within and peace without". The PPP pledges to give Pakistan and the region "peace within and peace without" with honour and dignity.

Foreign Policy

The Pakistan People's Party opposes terrorism and will continue the policy of the present regime to ally itself against the forces of terror.

Good Relations with its Neighbours

The PPP seeks good neighbourly relations with its neighbours.

The PPP, without prejudice to the UN Security Council Resolutions, supports open and safe borders at the Line of Control to socially unite the Kashmiri people. It notes that India and China have a border disputer and yet enjoy tension free relations. It seeks to reduce tensions with India through peaceful negotiations to outstanding disputes and issues.

South Asian Free Trade Zone

The PPP supports a South Asian Free Trade Zone. It believes that such a zone can enhance markets and job opportunities as well as enable the South Asian countries to formulate consensus views for World Trade Organisation and other international bodies that are coming into being to ensure that they are supportive of the rights of the people of South Asia.

War Against Terror

The war against terror focuses attention on the danger of rogue elements accessing nuclear systems of countries with inadequate command and control systems. The nuclear control and command centres as well as nuclear safety measures will be ensured by the PPP government to allay international fears and safeguard the nuclear assets.

PPP will continue to cement and enhance relations with Pakistan's traditional friends.

5

Her Speeches and Interviews

Introduction

Remarks at a Joint Appearance with U.S. President Bill Clinton by Benazir Bhutto (April 11, 1995)

Mr. President, ladies and gentlemen,

I'd like to begin by thanking the President for his kind words of support and encouragement.

Since 1989, my last visit to Washington, both the world and Pak-U.S. relations have undergone far-reaching changes. The post-Cold War era has brought into sharp focus the positive role that Pakistan, as a moderate, democratic, Islamic country of 130 million people, can play, and the fact that it is strategically located at the tri-junction of South Asia , Central Asia and the Gulf — a region of both political volatility and economic opportunity.

Globally, Pakistan is active in U.N. peacekeeping operations. They are on the forefront of the fight against international terrorism, narcotics, illegal immigration and counterfeit currency. They remain committed to the control and elimination of weapons of mass destruction, as well as the delivery systems on a regional, equitable and non-discriminatory basis.

Since 1993, concerted efforts by Pakistan and the United States to broaden the base of bilateral relations have resulted in steady progress. In September 1994, in a symbolic gesture, the United States granted Pakistan about $10 million in support for population planning. This was announced by the Vice President at the Cairo Summit on population planning. This was followed by the presidential mission, led by Energy Secretary Hazel O'Leary, which resulted in agreement worth $4.6 billion being signed. And, now, during my visit here, we are grateful to the administration and the Cabinet Secretaries for having helped us sign $6 billion more of agreements between Pakistan and the United States.

During the Defense Secretary's visit to Pakistan in January 1995, our countries decided to revive the Pakistan-United States Defense Consultative Group. And more recently, we had the First Lady and the First Daughter visit Pakistan, and we had an opportunity to discuss women's issues and children's issues with the First Lady. And we found the First Daughter very knowledgeable. They found Chelsea very knowledgeable on Islamic issues. I'm delighted to learn from the President that Chelsea is studying Islamic history and has also actually read our Holy Book, the Koran Shariah.

I'm delighted to have accepted President Clinton's invitation to Washington . This is the first visit by a Pakistani's Chief Executive in six years. President Clinton and I covered a wide range of subjects, including Kashmir, Afghanistan, Central Asia, Gulf, Pakistan-India relations, nuclear proliferation, U.N. peacekeeping, terrorism and narcotics.

I briefed him about corporate America's interest in Pakistan, which has resulted in the signing of $12 billion worth of MOUs in the last 17 months since our government took office. I urged an early resolution of the core issue of Kashmir, which poses a great threat to peace and security in our region. It has retarded progress on all issues, including nuclear and missile proliferation. A just and durable solution is the need of the hour, based on the wishes of the Kashmiri people, as envisaged in the Security Council resolutions. Pakistan remains committed to engage in a substantive dialogue with India to resolve this dispute, but not in a charade that can be used by our neighbour to mislead the international community. I am happy to note that the United States recognizes Kashmir as disputed territory and maintains that a durable solution can only be based on the will of the Kashmiri people.

Pakistan asked for a reassessment of the Pressler Amendment, which places discriminatory sanctions on Pakistan. In our view, this amendment has been a disincentive for a regional solution to the proliferation issue. Pakistan has requested the President and the administration to resolve the problem of our equipment worth $1.4 billion, which is held up. I am encouraged by my discussions with the President this morning and the understanding that he has shown for Pakistan's position. I welcome the Clinton administration's decision to work with Congress to revise the Pressler Amendment.

Thank you, Mr. President.

Democracy and Internationalism: Post Iraq. The World Political Forum (May 19, 2003), Turin, Italy

With Iraq divided into American, British and Polish controlled zones, we gather together in Turin at an extraordinary and difficult time. Whatever our own views on the path leading to the recent Iraq War, it is time to look forward.

It is time to assess the new world reality.

The post-Iraq international situation gives an opportunity to look for ways to promote the cause of democratization, human rights and the global community to which we are all committed.

Many in the international community felt uncomfortable with a war without United Nations sanction.

Demonstrations for peace broke out in the heart of Europe, at times larger than demonstrations within the Muslim world.

- No one likes war.
- No one likes repression either.
- Western societies absorb dissent.

Non-Western societies are yet to deal with the challenge of those victimized, persecuted, imprisoned, tortured and exiled because of their political views.

This community of the disaffected and the disenfranchised played a pivotal role both in Afghanistan and Iraq.

In Kabul and Baghdad, popular voices of the people were denied political space. They formed the political front for a war to reclaim their own land.

Countries descend into the darkness of international terrorism and state terrorism when pluralism is disrupted, when diversity is suppressed, when one man directs the destiny of millions, be it a Mullah Omar or Saddam Hussain or other dictators.

America's President George Bush justified war claiming:

"Men and women in every culture need liberty like they need food and water and air.

Everywhere that freedom arrives, humanity rejoices; and everywhere that freedom stirs, let tyrants fear."

Post Iraq, tyrants should fear.

It is troubling that some of those tyrants still feel little fear. Sadly, some of them are still close allies of Washington. In the case of Pakistan, a repressive regime exiles the popular opposition, imprisons dissidents and rigs elections.

In the post-Iraq world that dawned this April, the words rationalizing the Iraq war can be used to press all nations, and especially Washington, to make consistent application of democratic principles the essence of internationalism in this new millennium.

There were moments in recent history where historic moments were squandered. When the moving finger of history writes of the end of the 20th century, it will write of the international community's failure to reinforce the democratic breakthrough that the end of communism brought as the era's greatest missed opportunities.

I recall speaking to European Parliaments, to the Congress of the United States proclaiming that the era of the dictator was over, that militaries all over the world had finally returned to their barracks, that democracy was blooming on every continent.

In retrospect, I fear it was merely a mirage. The forces of real politic were waiting to collide with the ideology of democracy. They proclaimed a new moral era, but actually constructed an era of moral relativity. And ladies and gentlemen, selective morality is, by its very definition, immoral.

Their standards are inconsistent and our policies selective. Those that decry dictatorship in Burma are silent about tyranny elsewhere. Those decrying dictatorship in Iraq, stay close to dictators in Pakistan. Many in this room rightfully demand self-determination in Palestine, but are less vocal about the rights of the Kashmiri people.

In this age of moral relativism, political standards vary according to political expediency and economic imperatives. Democracy for Iraq, but dictatorship just miles away. Iraqi violations of UN resolutions bring a strong response. Violations of UN resolutions in the Middle East or in South Asia draw a less vocal reaction.

They evaluate national security by hardened borders and tanks and missiles. But true security is linked to the fight for economic justice that will liberate nations; true security is linked to the fight against famine and AIDs; true security means protecting the environment from pollution and desecration.

No matter how great and powerful a nation may be, true leadership is more than military action. It is leading the fight against AIDS, against hunger, against poverty, against racism, and for women, the fight for justice.

Ladies and gentlemen, the post-Iraq world situation allows us to focus once again on the principle of freedom. This time it must be more than rhetoric that is exploited in pursuit of limited, foreign policy objectives.

I remember a time when the world walked from Afghanistan after the defeat of the Soviets in 1989.

The fundamental mistake was that we were not consistently committed to the values of freedom, democracy and self-determination that ultimately undermine terrorism. The result was Taliban dictatorship, Al-Qaeda and terrorism.

Dictatorship doesn't constrain fundamentalism or terrorism. It provokes it. The goal of rational foreign policy must always be to simultaneously promote stability and to strengthen democratic values.

The stakes are high. Every war in the South Asian subcontinent from where I come started when my country was under a military dictator or one of its civilian surrogates. I do not know of a single case when a democratic country has gone to war against another democratic country.

Dictators are not accountable and do not need a popular mandate behind their policies.

The tragedy of Iraq is that Saddam Hussain spurned all offers of a peaceful transition from his regime to a democratic one. None dared tell him that he could not win a military war against American technology.

None dared criticize his flawed strategy of a prolonged guerrilla conflict with house to house fighting in Iraq's cities to force Washington into a ceasefire while he remained in control.

Dictators are cut off from reality by sycophants too scared to tell them the truth allowing for miscalculations that innocent people pay for in lives.

Democracies are different. Democratic leaders are accountable before the Parliament, the press and the people. Democratic governments must provide for the public welfare, must provide schools and hospitals, health and housing. Dictatorships need not. They rely on unaccountable secret services and are free to divert resources to schemes that parliamentary scrutiny simply would not permit.

History has taught us the very hard lesson that when democratic states turn against democracy, they turn against themselves.

Ladies and Gentlemen,

The international press has speculated about Islamabad's support to North Korea's nuclear programme. Islamabad denies the charges.

Even though Islamabad is a key ally of the US in the war against terrorism, Pakistani citizens are finger printed and photographed when they visit America.

Military dictator General Musharaf promised the world community he would seal the borders with Afghanistan to prevent fleeing Al Qaeda from slipping into Pakistan. Yet scores made their way into the country as the recent arrests by the FBI demonstrate.

Ladies and Gentlemen,

I believe a democratic Pakistan is the best guarantee of respect and dignity for the people of Pakistan. I believe that a democratic Pakistan living by the rule of law within and without is the best guarantee of the triumph of moderation and modernity amongst one billion Muslims at the crossroads of our history.

These are difficult times. They stand at the crossroads of a new world order. They witness the dawn of a uni-polar world environment where wars can take place with the coalition of the willing. They witness disunity in the United Nations Security Council, in NATO, in Europe and in the Muslim world.

They can remember that the future is in our hands. As the European philosopher Goethe once wrote, "Freedom must be reinvented in every generation."

Unipolarism can lead to unilateralism. As power shifts to new paradigms the challenge is to find ways where the voices of the rest of the world community can also be heard effectively.

This is our turn to reinvent freedom.

And we shall prevail.

Thank you ladies and gentlemen.

Victims of Terrorism, Speech delivered by Benazir Bhutto in the US (December 2002)

I am pleased to come before you at the season of the year when Christmas, Eid and Hanukah coincide. Maybe in this week of holidays that celebrate renewal, hope, faith and peace, we can begin to move away from the precipice of disaster that I fear the world finds itself in December of 2002.

I know you are here primarily to learn from my experiences throughout my career that you may be able to apply to your own lives, responsibilities and careers. I intend to address those points.

But these are very special times. These are very dangerous times. These are times of misperceptions and confusion. I want to take part of the time to share with you some thoughts about the extraordinary state of the world.

First let us address the issue of terrorism, Islam and the West. Terrorism and fanaticism will not succeed unless we fall into the psychopaths' trap. Professor Samuel Huntington of Harvard wrote of an inevitable clash of civilization between the West and the Islamic world.

I argue that this clash is far from inevitable, unless we make it so.

There is nothing in the precepts of Islam that make it inconsistent with Judeo-Christian values. In the Holy Book, Abraham is our father, just as Moses and Jesus are our prophets.

There will only be a clash of civilizations if we allow ignorance and fanaticism to take control, to shape the agenda and to shape the debate.

Osama and his men use commercial airliners as bombs against cities and symbols to provoke the clash of cultures under which they will thrive.

I am not unfamiliar with the terrorists of Al Qeda.

I know them well; I know how they operate, how they think and I know what they want.

As Prime Minister of Pakistan, I stood up to them. I battled with many of these same criminals, including

Osama Bin Laden himself. I took them on, and often paid a price.

During the Afghan-Soviet war, my country became the breeding ground for their psycho-political religious manipulation and exploitation. Hiding under the cloak of religion, they preached a message that would enslave not liberate, teach children not to write but rather to hate, keep people hopeless and desperate, bitter, xenophobic and paranoid.

I closed their so-called universities. I disarmed their Madrassas, their sham primary schools that do not teach children literature, science or mathematics but rather turn children into fanatics and criminals. I tried to restore law and order to our cities under incessant assault from terrorist attack.

My government tracked down and extradited the terrorists, like Ramzi Youseff, who had exported death and destruction to New York in the 1990s.

They struck back at my allies and me. They destroyed the Egyptian Embassy in Islamabad. They burned our National Assembly, hijacked school buses, gunned down diplomats and businessmen in the streets of Karachi and Lahore, and organized and financed schemes to topple my government.

As a woman, I was their enemy.

As a democrat, I was their opposite. But above all, as someone who offered hope to our people education, jobs, communication and modernity I was a dangerous obstacle to the forces of hate.

I took them on with my eyes open. I knew they would strike back, just as we expect that these fanatics to try and strike again in America.

Despite the personal and political price I paid over the years, my only regret is that we were unable to destroy them completely, before they rained terror on America.

Peace is often difficult to achieve, and even more difficult to maintain. The words on the Korean War Memorial on Washington's great mall never have rung more true.

"Freedom is not free.".

These terrorists' greatest fear is the spread of information, social equality and democracy. These three principles suffocate terrorism.

These three goals guided my years as prime minister. Maybe this could explain the two assassination attempts against me by Al Queda.

My government heralded the information age by introducing fax machines, digital pagers, optic fiber communications, cellular telephones, satellite dishes, computers, Internet, e-mail and even CNN into Pakistan.

Under my government Pakistan integrated into the global economy that the fanatics so fear. They became one of the ten emerging capital markets of the world, attracting billions of dollars in foreign investment, particularly in power generation. They eradicated polio in our country. They dramatically reduced infant mortality.

WHO

Despite the constraints of a political system rigged against democrats, and a social system biased against women, as Prime Minister of Pakistan I used my office to reverse centuries of discrimination against women.

My tenure was a textbook affirmative action programme against gender discrimination.

They increased literacy by one-third, even more dramatically among girls.

They built over 30,000 primary and secondary schools, targeting rural Pakistan. Their education program targeting girls and rural areas has been dismantled by the military junta.

They brought down the population growth rate by establishing women's health clinics in thousands of communities across our Nation.

They outlawed domestic violence and established special women's police forces to protect and defend the women of Pakistan.

They appointed women judges to our nation's benches for the first time in our history.

They instituted a new programme of hiring women police officers to investigate crimes of domestic violence against the women of Pakistan. That special police force has been dismantled.

I systematically appointed women judges to the courts of the land. That affirmative action programme for women in the judiciary has been dismantled.

I condemned, as state police, the honour killing, by members of their own families, of women who had been raped. The military junta is now silent to these abominations.

I condemned and sought to reverse the unspeakable prosecution of women raped and then tried for the crime of adultery, a perversion of justice that affronts the civilized world. The military junta uses this abomination as a means to solidify support among extremists.

I encouraged women's and girls' participation in sports, nationally and internationally, by lifting the ban on women's participation in sport. I persuaded the armed forces and security services to hire women in their institutions.

PIA Pilot

I created a special Women's Development Bank to guarantee small business loans to women entrepreneurs, because I firmly believed that economic justice would build political justice. It was a bank run by women for women, although men were allowed to keep their money in it.

Case-by-case, issue-by-issue, policy-by-policy, the military junta that rules Pakistan with an iron fist undermines policies aimed at ameliorating the role and rights of women in Pakistani society.

The women of Pakistan cannot be expected to struggle alone against the forces of discrimination, exploitation and manipulation.

I recall the words of Dante who reminded us that "the hottest place in Hell is reserved for those who remain neutral in times of moral crisis."

To the fanatics and the extremists, we became the enemy, the threat, and the obstacle. To Islam at the crossroads, a modern Pakistan was one fork in the road, fanaticism and ignorance the other.

Islam is committed to tolerance and equality, and it is committed by Koranic definition to the principles of democracy. The Holy Book says that Islamic society is contingent on and I quote "mutual advise through mutual discussions on an equal footing."

Sadly, most Muslim countries are dictatorships, contrary to what Islam teaches. The denial of democracy shifts opposition from the political class to the mosque. This play into hands of militants and extremists. They can canvass to a captive audience.

In Islam, dictatorship is never condoned, nor is cruelty. Beating, torturing and humiliating women is unIslamic. Denying education to girls violates the very first word of the Holy Book: "Read." According to our religion, those who commit cruel acts are condemned to destruction.

Sometimes tragedy can lead to resurrection of hope and spirit. As America and the civilized world respond to the most terrible terrorist attack in history, we must remember the lessons of history and not repeat the mistakes of the past.

Osama Bin Ladin did not emerge like whole cloth from a nightmare. His depravity was long in the making, and there were errors of omission and commission that must never be repeated.

Afghanistan is a tragic case in point of how retreating from the principles of human rights and democracy can have the most tragic unanticipated consequences.

In the closing days of the Soviet occupation of Afghanistan, during a State Visit to America I cautioned that US policy to defeat the Soviets had empowered and emboldened the most fanatical, extremist elements of the Afghan seven-faction Mujahadeen at the expense of the moderates, creating a "Frankenstein" that could come back to haunt us in the future.

The overall policy of standing against Soviet aggression in Afghanistan was right. Yet the early decisions to arm, train, supply and legitimize the most extreme fanatics sowed the seeds for the 21st century terrorism that is now swirling around us. In America and Pakistan's combined and admirable zeal to end the Soviet occupation, we failed to plan or work for a post-war Afghanistan built on democratic principles of coalition, consensus and cooperation.

The fundamental mistake, which contributed to a long-term historical calamity, was that we were not consistently committed to the values of freedom, democracy, social equality and self-determination that ultimately undermine the basic tenets of terrorism.

Short-term battlefield strategy is often myopic, as the anarchy, civil war and Taliban terror in Afghanistan so painfully proves. Just as democracies do not make war against other democracies, democracies also do not sponsor international terrorism.

The goal of the international community's foreign policy agenda must always be to simultaneously promote stability and to strengthen democratic values.

Not selectively but universally.

Not when it is convenient but rather because it is right.

General Musharraf made the correct decision to stand with America at this moment of crisis. But the United States and the rest of the world must remember that Pakistan has an extra-constitutional military government with no democratic legitimacy.

This is tragic, for a democratic Pakistan is America' best guarantee of the triumph of moderation and modernity among one billion Muslims at the crossroads of our history.

The alternative of a long-term nuclear-armed Pakistani dictatorship has consequences that could make September 11th look like a mere prelude to an even more horrific future for the civilized world.

This is not the simple world we dreamed of with the end of the Cold War. And mine is not the simple life I dreamed of growing up in Pakistan and going to school at Harvard and Oxford.

The gauntlet of leadership was thrown down before me. I had no choice but to pick it up. But it has often been very difficult, often very sad. Leadership is not easy. It is never meant to be easy. It is born of a passion, and it is a commitment, a commitment to an idea, to principles, to fundamental human values.

It has not always been an easy life for me, or for my family. But this is nothing new, really. Women have always had to make difficult choices, often choices that men are not been forced to make. And we must live with the consequences, for better or worse.

Those of us in positions of responsibility understand this special, unique and extraordinary moment in history. They fight for all the women who came before us who gave us this opportunity. And most of all, we do it for all women who will come after us the baby girls yet unborn! As a child of my age, in the late sixties, I was influenced by the social ferment around me. The worldwide student movement, from Rawalpindi, to Washington, was important factors in my youth. The fight against apartheid shaped the ferocity of my commitment to stand up for principle. The burgeoning movement for women's rights empowered and emboldened me.

As an Asian at Harvard, I joined up with American students to protest a war that they thought was unjust and did not want to fight.

These important steps helped shape my outlook on life, helped me focus on fighting injustice, promoting freedom and safeguarding the rights of the weak and dispossessed. But above all, in America during the Watergate crises I saw the awesome power of the people to change policies, change leaders, and change history.

From Harvard I went to Oxford, where the British politician Enoch Powell was threatening to throw all Asians into the sea.

While I was at Oxford, the Conservative Party chose a woman, Margaret Thatcher, as the Leader of Opposition.

The idea of the first female British Prime Minister became an intense topic for student discussions.

At Oxford, I was the first female foreigner to be elected as President of the Oxford Union.

The Oxford Union reflects the British Parliament.

It was there that I learned to debate, slowly gaining confidence before an audience.

I had been told that as a foreigner, I could not win the Presidency and should not run.

I had been told that as a woman, I could not win, and should not run. But I did run and did win and overcame my fear of losing. I learned to overcome fear and to take risks. I learned never to give in when the task seemed formidable or impossible.

What has always been clear to me is that the extraordinary educational opportunities I had gave me a range of life and career options denied to most women, and certainly almost all women of the developing world.

My own experiences at Harvard and Oxford made it clear to me that only educational opportunity promotes empowerment for women.

If women are truly to be defined by themselves and their own accomplishments and abilities, they need the level of education that empowers them. Education leads to the kind of financial independence that causes women to break the shackles of being only a man's daughter or a man's wife.

Toba Tek Singh

As the Prime Minister of Pakistan I appeared before an historic Joint Session of the United States Congress in 1989.

In that address, the most meaningful line to me was my simple message to the women of America, my message to the women of the world. Three simple, powerful words: YES YOU CAN!

I urge women all over the world not to accept the status quo, not to accept "no" for an answer. It is critical that women

— whether in London or Kabul — refuse to accept traditional roles and traditional constraints.

Acquiescing to a tradition dictated by men, a tradition of subjugation of mothers and daughters can no longer be accepted. In the West and in the East, we must stand up and reject the notion that leadership and femininity are contradictory.

I recall the words of Lady Margaret Thatcher. "When a woman is strong, she is pushy. But when a man is strong...ah...he is a great leader!"

They've made progress; we've smashed many glass ceilings. But there are thousands left to break, many battles left to fight.

The greatest obstacles to progress for women in the third millennium is the bigotry of men, and nowhere is that bigotry more venal than in the Taliban and the fanatics that have declared war on the civilized world.

They fight against terrorism, and the bigotry and intolerance that will confine and constrain and victimize in the generations ahead.

Victimization of significant elements of society and the concept of long-term peace are mutually exclusive.

The denial of human rights is a bomb that ultimately explodes.

These are difficult times. Freedom is under assault. Democracy is under assault. Criminal terrorists hijack my religion just as they hijack America's planes.

The solutions will not be quick or simple. But if we maintain our commitment to the principles that define us the principles of racial, gender and religious equality, the principles of political pluralism and tolerance, and the principles of peaceful change through democracy we shall in the end prevail.

In addressing the new exigencies of the new century, we could translate dynamic religion into a living reality. Muslim societies need to learn to live by the true spirit of Islam, not only by its rituals.

Those who are ignorant of Islam, could cast aside their preconceptions about the role of women in our religion.

Contrary to what many believe, Islam embraces a rich variety of political, social and cultural traditions. The fundamental ethos of Islam is tolerance, dialogue and democracy. Just as in Christianity and Judaism, we must always be on guard for those who use the Muslim Holy Book for their own narrow political ends, who will distort the essence of pluralism and tolerance for their own extremist agendas.

These manipulators, distorters and bigots exist all over the world, but nowhere were they more dangerous and destructive than the last years of the Taliban era in Afghanistan.

And most central to the Taliban perversion was its concept and treatment of women.

For the Taliban, and other extremists throughout the Muslim world, refute the central ethos of Islam which is equality, especially equality between the sexes. I find Islam in its writings, respectful of the role of women in society. It is this tradition of Islam that empowered me, strengthened me, and emboldened me.

It is this tradition of Islam that allowed me my battle for political and human rights. It strengthens me today in this hour of crisis for my family, my nation and myself.

Today in Pakistan, the veil of repression has descended across our people.

The cause of human rights is being set back decades.

But the cause of women's rights, I am sad to say, is being set back a century.

My immediate successor's attempt to turn back the clock on women's rights, on liberal society, on pluralistic democracy focused on me, on destroying me politically at home and destroying my reputation abroad.

They have become accustomed to attempts to use the politics of personal destruction to turn back the course of democracy, human rights and women's rights in our homeland. It didn't work then and it will not work now.

Despite the Musharraf regime's support of the international war against terrorism, this military junta, like its Martial law predecessors of the past, is attempting to use the teaching of Islam as an excuse to subjugate women, deny freedom, destroy a free press, dominate NGOs, break up political parties, decimate the judiciary, and restore the iron hand of dictatorship to the land.

For me, it is particularly heartbreaking, as the military regime dismantles the array of special programmes that I instituted in my two terms as Prime Minister to raise the quality of life of women in Pakistan. Unfortunately, hiding under the aura of international cooperation on terrorism, the current regime in Islamabad continues to terrorize its own women. A world focused on the destruction of the Al Qaeda network has neither the interest nor the knowledge to investigate the human rights abuses in a "coalition" member.

And thus the causes of women's rights, human rights, press freedom and democracy fall backwards into the dark chasms of a past era.

Yet I see great progress looming as the forces that shape the new century and the new millennium come together around the world.

It is a confluence of energy committed to universal social, economic and political values this triad definition of comprehensive human rights for the future.

It is a confluence of ideology that must shape a world free from exploitation and maltreatment of women, a world in which women have opportunities to rise to the highest level in politics, business, diplomacy, and other spheres of life.

The new century must, for once and for all, exclude even the notion of battered women.

It must be an era where honour and dignity are protected in peace, and in war, where women have economic freedom and independence, where women are not defined by their fathers or husbands, but by their own achievements, where they are equal partners in peace and development.

Even as we catalogue, organize and hopefully attain our goals, step by step, all of those around the world who are committed to the common causes of human rights, women's rights and peace, must be vigilant.

As in Pakistan today, repressive forces always stand ready to exploit the moment and push us back into the past.

It seems that the words of Goethe continue to resonate: "freedom has be re-made and re-earned in every generation."

Dear Guests,

In the time it took for me to speak to you today, over one thousand children starved to death on this planet.

As long as these basic violations of human rights are allowed to continue, none of us regardless of where we live, regardless of how elegant or civilized our life-styles, regardless of our own personal circumstances and comforts are free.

My father, Prime Minister Zulfiqar Ali Bhutto, was toppled and ultimately murdered by the forces of dictatorship and extremism two decades ago. I recall vividly those dark and tragic days, with my father languishing in a dark prison, living in the most inhumane conditions, with the world helpless to stop his murder.

But he remained courageous to the end, even in the hours before his death.

I want to end this monograph with the words that he ended his last letter to me, quoting Robert F. Kennedy, himself a victim of assassination, commenting on the poetry of Alfred Lord Tennyson. Despite the crisis we live under today, these words set the tone for a new and brighter future.

In 1979, from the horror of his death cell, my father wrote:

"Every generation has a central concern, whether to end war, erase racial injustice, or improve the conditions of working people. The people demand a government that speaks directly and honestly to its citizens. The possibilities are too great, the stakes too high, to bequeath to the coming generation only the prophetic lament of Tennyson "Ah, what shall I be at fifty"

If there is anything that I can truly share from my life that applies to yours, it is the classic quote Shakespeare's Hamlet, "to thine own self be true."

In politics and business, in art and in the academy, there will always be pressures to do what is convenient, the path of least resistance, what is safe and conservative.

But leadership is not rooted in safety; it rather is a product of boldness.

Do not be timid.

And do not surround yourself with those who are timid.

Don't do what is necessarily popular, do what is right.

It is sad that modern leaders often take public opinion polls to decide on courses of policy.

Sixty years ago, a truly great leader, American President Franklin Delano Roosevelt, also took polls.

But he didn't take polls to determine what course to follow.

On the contrary, he took polls to find out where the people were so that he would know how to educate them to stand with him to do what was right.

Leaders lead, remember that.

Convince, educate, bring people around to do what is moral, to do what is right, to do what is necessary.

Whether it is in politics or business, don't be afraid to stand out and stand up.

Ladies and gentlemen, go forth and lead. Good luck.

Interviews

Interview of Mohtarma Benazir Bhutto

Karen Yopr

1. What do you think of Lt. Gen. Ashfaque Kiani? He's a close ally of Musharraf. Does that bother you?

Ans: Lt General Kiani has a reputation as a professional officer which is what the armed forces and Pakistan need.

2. The army controls everything from arms to businesses and there are those who are supporting extremism and terrorism. How would you be able to handle and control the Army?

Ans: Their first step is to separate the offices of army chief and the President. General Musharaf has now given an undertaking to the Supreme Court of Pakistan that he will retire as army chief after the presidential elections this October. Under the present military doctored Constitution, the armed forces come under the President. The political parties would need to unite to bring control of the armed forces back to Parliament for reform to take place. PPP has signed a Charter of Democracy calling upon political parties to make the members of the armed forces answerable to Parliament, as they are in Washington, London and France, for greater transparency and accountability.

3. What would be your ideal amendment to the Constitution, if you return to power?

Ans: To prevent a return to the dysfunctional democracy of the nineties, it is important to do away with the powers of the president to dismiss an elected parliament in his discretion. Secondly, there are other issues like lifting the military imposed ban on a twice elected prime minister contesting election for a third time for prime minister, appointment of Governors, members of the judiciary and Election Commission. The Charter of Democracy spells out the changes needed.

4. You've mentioned about the package deal with Musharraf: balance of power, reforms for a fair election, lifting the ban on a twice-elected prime minister. When do you expect these to happen and how so?

Ans: These issues are part of our negotiations and will happen in a phased manner. Some steps have already been taken like arrangements for shedding military uniform, the counting of ballots, stopping horse trading by preventing arrest of parliamentarians without permission of an Ethics Committee, end to political victimization and national reconciliation. I hope other issues like eligibility of Prime

Ministerial candidates and balance of power between parliament and presidency will also be resolved in due course.

5. Elaborate on what does "a power-sharing" deal means? Would this include the Army as well since Musharraf has a hold on them?

Ans: The PPP negotiations are not to share power but to restore democracy through the holding of fair, free and impartial elections where civilians govern and people are the masters of their own destiny.

6. Being in self-exile for 8 years, what has changed inside on a person (as a mother and wife) and professional level (as a politician)?

Ans: Adversity has tempered my character. My husband was in jail in Pakistan for 8 years without a conviction and I had to bring up small children as single parent in exile besides looking after my ailing mother. Scores of members of my party were killed. They paid a heavy price for democracy. This experience has strengthened my commitment for building a tolerant society which respects human rights, allows a free media, has a transparent and corruption free government which tackles the social and economic issues of the people, brings peace internally by undermining the forces of extremism and builds peace regionally.

7. How would you run the country now in comparison to your previous tenures? Which issues would you give priority?

Ans: I would seek reconciliation, peace, ending militancy, eradicating poverty, building institutions of civil rule and democracy, spreading education and providing hope to the people of Pakistan for a better future.

8. You mentioned before that you'd better controls in the tribal areas when you were in office. Things have certainly changed during the past years — 9/11 and the rising inflation rate and terrorism in the country. How do you expect to tackle an uphill task after being out of action for 8 years?

Ans: The military government has relied solely on the use of force in dealing with extremism in the tribal areas. They believe that alongside the use of force, we also need to take political steps and improve the socio-economic conditions of the people in the tribal area. Poverty and social isolation also breed militancy. They will address issues of poverty and social isolation in the tribal areas. My Party has already filed a constitutional petition in the Supreme Court seeking the extension of Political Parties Act to the tribal areas. They want to bring the people of the tribal areas into the twenty first century and make them stake-holders in fighting militancy and extremism. They would interrupt the flow of drug funds that finance militancy as well as spread education and employment.

9. It was understood that you tried to strike a deal with the Army. How will you go with your deal with Musharraf?

Ans: I am not striking any deal with the Army. I am looking at transition to democracy in which the Parliament is sovereign and the military performs its constitutionally ordained duties.

10. Your take on American funds to Pakistan for the war on terror. Increasingly, there is an anti-American sentiment among Pakistanis because the country's leaders continue to be dictated by the American government. Do you think the country still needs aid to fight terror? What would you have done?

Ans: Terrorism is a threat to the internal unity and integrity of Pakistan. Unless it is eliminated, God forbid, Pakistan could disintegrate and its people suffer bloodshed and civil war. A PPP government will cooperate with the international community in the fight on terror to save Pakistan and bring regional security for a safer world.

11. Observers said the power marriage between you and Musharraf will not last due to conflicting interests, management styles and personalities. What is your comment?

Ans: It is for the people to decide who will govern them. However, unless the Constitution clearly spells out the responsibilities of the President and Parliament, no government will survive irrespective of the management styles and personalities of the persons involved. The dismissals of earlier governments including that of Prime Minister Junejo and Prime Minister Nawaz prove the point. I argue for a Constitution that permits for stability.

12. Critiques said that you do not have the slightest clue as to how a soldier gets sandwiched between his oath of a soldier and his own conscience while killing Muslim brothers. What is your comment?

Ans: I would not like to see the Pakistan army kill Muslims or non-Muslims whether it is in East Pakistan, Baluchistan, Karachi or the tribal areas of Pakistan. However, I would like to see the Pakistan army defend the unity and territorial integrity of Pakistan and come in aid of civil power to protect the lives, liberty and livelihood of the people of Pakistan whenever it is under threat.

"Musharraf Can't Become President"

Prabhu Chawla

For seven long years Benazir Bhutto has been dreaming of returning to Pakistan, the country she has served as prime minister twice. As she began finalising the details of her impending return to her homeland, the excitement was laced with uncertainty. Not surprising, since last week another former prime minister, Nawaz Sharif, who too was on a homecoming after eight years, was bundled from one airplane to another and banished to Jeddah in Saudi Arabia. The Pakistan People's Party (PPP) leader spoke to INDIA TODAY Editor Prabhu Chawla for Aaj Tak. Excerpts from the interview:

Q. So how do you feel about your impending departure for home?

A. I am very excited. Seven years is a long time and I am wondering what changes have taken place.

Q. What do you expect? A red carpet or the reception that Sharif got?

A. I don't know how I will be received. But I am not in the same boat as him. He has been convicted by the court of law and sentenced for treason and tax evasion. He had traded his imprisonment for a 10-year exile in Saudi Arabia with his family and this involved foreign guarantees. I was given the same offer. But I refused. So unlike Nawaz Sharif, I cannot be put on a plane and sent out.

Q. But the Government will not allow you also to return as there are charges pending against you.

A. The corruption charges against me have not been withdrawn. As far as I am concerned, I am out on bail and should not be arrested. I stayed out so I would not lose my freedom of expression, freedom of speech, freedom of movement and association.

Q. Is there an agreement with General Musharraf that he would be your presidential choice and you will be his prime minister?

A. The discussion or transition to democracy has not been successful so far. I am going back in an uncertain environment.

Q. Is there any deal with him?

A. Of course not. Please do not use this word. It is unfair to my long history of suffering.

Q. I know you will not admit it but you went to Abu Dhabi to meet him.

A. That was a non-meeting.

Q. Non-meeting or no meeting.

A. Neither side has officially admitted to the meeting. But contacts between the regime and PPP have been taking place since 1999.

Q. General Musharraf's popularity is on the wane and he needs a civilian face to stay in power. Are you willing to protect him?

A. Whether he needs someone to protect him or not, only he can answer.

But the people of Pakistan need someone to fight for their rights.

Q. You are Benazir Bhutto, who is in exile, facing persecution and whose father was executed. Is it right on your part to compromise with someone who has deposed an elected prime minister?

A. I cannot compromise. I am seeking the restoration of democracy.

Q. Prime ministers rarely survive their full term in Pakistan. You yourself were dismissed twice. Is there something wrong with the DNA of Pakistan which makes military rulers throw out elected rulers?

A. I feel very upset to hear that there is something wrong with the DNA of Pakistan. Unfortunately, the military has impeded the democratic growth of Pakistan, unlike in India where you have a democracy and a peaceful transfer of power. India is also emerging as an economic powerhouse and is a force to reckon with on the world stage.

Q. But we have the same blood. They are only divided by geography.

A. Because of the military, Pakistan has not developed institutions or has had a stable environment where growth can take place.

Q. Have you set any pre-conditions for your return to Pakistan?

A. There are no agreements. I am going back unconditionally.

Q. You have been holding talks.

A. Everybody is talking. Sharif has been talking since 2000, otherwise how could he go to Saudi Arabia?

Q. Will you allow Musharraf to continue as President?

A. There has been a dialogue, but there has been no agreement. The dialogue is not about personalities but about holding of free and fair elections to get civilians in power.

Q. If Musharraf gives up the uniform, can he be the President?

A. First, this question is premature. Second, it is not for me to choose the President. The people will decide.

Q. Will your party support Musharraf if he stays in uniform?

A. They oppose a unformed presidency.

Q. What comes first? Kashmir or uniform?

A. That's a good question.

Q. You are dodging the issue.

A. No, I am not. It is not based on one element. If today, for example, Musharraf announces that he will give up the uniform, it doesn't mean there will be an agreement. Same if he were to lift the ban on twice-elected prime ministers from contesting.

Q. You have not defined the transition of democracy.

A. They are for holding of free and fair elections.

Q. In India, we cannot make a general the President under our Constitution.

A. In your country, you make even a nuclear scientist the President. If we did something like that in Pakistan, there would be utter chaos.

Q. But our nuclear scientists do not sell state secrets abroad. Why don't you make a rule that prohibits generals from becoming President?

A. I think you are right. In Pakistan, we make rules but the military does not allow us to implement them.

Q. Has Musharraf lost the will of the people?

A. Opinion polls suggest that.

Q. Should he go?

A. This is for the people to decide.

Q. You represent the people, don't you?

A. I am no Nostradamus. I cannot predict events.

Q. The judiciary has been very active in Pakistan.

A. Yes. Under the restored chief justice. They have great satisfaction that there is a check from the Supreme Court in disputed matters. But there are disputes over everything.

Q. Are you going to be a future prime minister or prisoner?

A. There are questions that don't have answers. Will elections be held? Will they be free and fair? Will opposition parties get together?

Q. The only permanent answer is that Musharraf will stay.

A. That is also uncertain. The question is if Musharraf is eligible to contest another term in office. According to the Constitution, as a former army chief, there's a two-year bar on a government servant to contest. So this issue will end up in courts.

Q. So you are saying Musharraf should give up the uniform, the ban on twice-elected prime ministers contesting elections should be lifted and ...

A. It is important that all corruption cases against party workers be lifted and immunity be given to them. This is in everyone's interest.

Q. Do you support Sharif's deportation?

A. The courts have to rule in this matter. Every citizen has the right to come back. But the other argument is that Sharif traded his rights to live in Pakistan for the dropping of charges against him.

Q. Is your fight against Sharif or Musharraf?

A. My fight is for democracy.

Q. But he has scored a symbolic victory over you.

A. I don't buy it. Very few people were present at the airport when he arrived. He made a mistake by making a deal, involving foreign parties and so on. But people can review mistakes. And I hope he will.

Q. People say America is playing the intermediary between you and Musharraf.

A. They are going back and forth in Pakistan in the larger interest of the war against terrorism.

Q. Are you not talking to them? Aren't you the US nominee for the prime ministership of Pakistan?

A. Of course, we have been talking to them. They talk to all parties. This is the nature of political discourse. They welcome their democratic support.

Q. But unlike you, Sharif is clear that he will not talk to a dictator.

A. I disagree, because he did talk.

Q. That was earlier.

A. They are told that he talked. He was supposed to be travelling on Gulf Air earlier, but he went on a state PIA plane later.

Q. Are you saying he had a secret deal with the Government?

A. I don't know.

Q. Will you become prime minister under Musharraf as President?

A. This will depend on the people of Pakistan if they get to vote in free and fair elections.

Q. Assume that the elections are fair.

A. I can't do so because of the ground realities. The point is Pakistan is in turmoil because of so many issues and no one knows the course. Things could lead to an emergency, a military rule and deferment of polls. Even the militant hardliners are frightened of democracy. They seem to have adopted a Minus 3 Formula now first it was opposition to me, then Sharif and now me, Sharif and Musharraf. The hardliners who formed the Mujahideen and became members of the Taliban and Al-Qaeda do not want the people to get back their rights because their agenda will be rolled back.

Q. So for you, restoration of democracy is more important than whether Musharraf stays in power or not.

A. No. For me, the right of the people to choose their leaders is most important.

Q. And is it none of your business whether Musharraf is chosen or not?

A. The question is whether he is eligible or not.

Q. You are also not eligible to become prime minister under the current laws.

A. Yes, but I can contest elections and Parliament can change the law.

Q. But you would like to become prime minister.

A. Yes. If people give me the mandate, it will be a great honour.

Q. In the event of your party coming to power, is your candidature for prime ministership certain?

A. Of course, my party has only one candidate.

Q. So your mission to Pakistan is to return as prime minister and restore democracy.

A. I can sit back and ask why should I take the risk? But I believe every Pakistani has the right to live in Pakistan

Mohtarma Bhutto addresses Middle East Institute in Washington

"The people of Pakistan want change. Change of systems, change of programmes, change from a climate of threat to one of stability and prosperity. They don't want to see the sham of 2002 repeated again, resulting in an illegitimate government that has no mandate to govern and fails to give security of life or economic growth that can provide hope and opportunity to those unemployed or living on the margins of poverty", former Prime Minister and Chairperson of Pakistan Peoples Party, Mohtarma Benazir Bhutto said this while speaking at the Middle East Institute, in Washington on September 25, 2007. A large number of opinion makers, intellectuals, scholars, lecturers and students attended the function. Former US ambassador to Pakistan, Wendy Chamberlain heads the Middle East Institute.

The former Prime Minister giving a detailed account of prevailing situation in Pakistan said, "It is a critical fork in the road between democracy and dictatorship and between moderation and extremism. In its resolution lies not only the future of Pakistan, but also its ability to contain the spread of militancy and extremism which now threatens the territorial integrity of Pakistan. Some argue that extremism can better be confronted by a military backed regime. It will not surprise you that I disagree with this view quite vigorously. I think it is a strategic miscalculation that has had a negative impact in the battle against violent fanaticism, posing grave dangers both to Pakistan and the larger world community. The attacks on the World Trade Towers, the Cole ship at Yemen, the embassies in Africa, the blasts in Bombay and in the Indian Parliament took place when I was in opposition".

Regarding the military regime's inability to control the spread of extremism in Pakistan, Mohtarma Benazir Bhutto said, "Large sections of Pakistan's tribal areas have been ceded to non-Pakistanis in the Taliban and Al-Qaeda militias. In fact, after defeat and demoralization following the fall of the Kabul, these violent elements have re-organized themselves under the shadow of the military regime. They attack NATO forces across the border in Afghanistan every day. They conduct suicide attacks within Pakistan killing innocent people. On September 20, 2007, Al – Qaeda declared war on the Pakistan army. Military dictatorship has fueled extremism. A democratically elected government enjoying the support of the people can bring peace to the people of Pakistan and eliminate extremism. Eliminate terrorism by taking extremism off the radar screen of the region. I was the civilian female leader of a democratic Pakistan that invested political capital in the tribal areas that a military regime has failed to control. As Prime Minister I brought the rule of law and the fruits of development to the people in the Federally Administered Tribal Areas. My government broke up the international drug cartel's militias that have now reasserted themselves under the Musharraf rule and are funding Al – Qaeda to have a narco-fiefdom. My administration brought the authority of the government and the rule of law to FATA in the 1990s. And we can do it again. I would also add that as Prime Minister I took the necessary steps to close down political madrassas whose curriculum taught hatred and para-military terrorist techniques. I did this before they became a threat to the world community. I considered them a threat to the stability, security and progress of the people of Pakistan. It is only dictatorships which have used the Islamic card to legitimize their rule at the expense of the neglected people of Pakistan. Dictatorships, lacking a popular base, need the religious card, played in one shape or another, to justify their stranglehold on power. They need a crisis to obtain international support, both political and financial. Extremists have never been able to achieve more than 11 per cent of the vote in a free election, and they will do worse, not better if free elections are held today. Dictatorship in Pakistan is not containing extremism, it is fueling. Each of Pakistan's four military dictatorships has assaulted the major infrastructural building blocks of democracy by attempting to marginalize political parties, dismantling NGO's and undermining civil society, by constraining labour and student unions, and allowing the intelligence agencies and government members to physically assault and intimidate the free press. Each military dictatorship has undermined the independent judiciary by sacking of judges. In the last twenty years, my government is the only one which has neither removed a Chief Justice nor attacked the premises of the Supreme Court."

Mohtarma Benazir Bhutto expressed grave concerns about the political element in Musharraf 's party that presided over the rise of extremism and said, "Dictatorships, by dismantling the infrastructure of democracy, allow the mosques to become the only outlet of political expression in Pakistan. The Musharraf regime has appointed extremists to head many of the mosques. For example, the head cleric of the Red Mosque in Islamabad, who led a mutiny in the summer of 2007, was appointed by the regime of General Musharraf. When he was caught smuggling weapons into Islamabad in 2004, he was released by the Minister of Religious Affairs. The same minister has twice defended suicide attacks before a Pakistani audience while retracting them for the international community. When Pakistanis gather to pray on Friday in the mosques they are often subjected to long lectures by radical clerics appointed by the government even as the government claims publicly to be against extremism. The voices of moderation are exiled or imprisoned. The voices of extremism are protected. Moderate and centrist political parties, thriving human and political rights NGOs, the media, and progressive leadership within our security and intelligence agencies must be brought together to confront extremists who pose the greatest internal threat to Pakistan. This is a battle that can only successfully be waged in a democratic Pakistan by a legitimate government that enjoys the support of the people. This is a battle that I am prepared to wage, to lead and to win."

Regarding dialogue with General Musharraf, she said, "The goal of my dialogue with Musharraf has never been personal. The goal was always to ensure that there be fair and free elections in Pakistan, pursuant to the Constitution, supervised by a robust team of international monitors and observers, as quickly as possible. My goal was quite literally to save democracy in Pakistan, to give democracy a chance to nurture and grow and strengthen."

On the issue of presidential election in Pakistan, she said, "Once General Musharraf files his nomination papers, the PPP would decide whether it would resign from the present Parliament or whether it would boycott the elections. While the PPP would not vote for General Musharraf as President from this Parliament unless there is a constitutional amendment, it would not resign if he took the necessary steps to show that he was moving towards fair elections and a level-playing field. If General Musharraf will retire from the post of Army Chief by October 5, given his pledge to retire before the year's end; second seek national reconciliation by passing an immunity law for those parliamentarians not proven guilty in the last decade; and third repeal the ban on a twice elected prime minister seeking office a law that he put into place contrary to the constitution; the PPP will not resign from the Assemblies. The Pakistan People's Party is holding a meeting with its ARD allies to decide this issue on October 3. Civil unrest is what the extremists want. Anarchy and chaos suit them.

The political element in Musharraf's party that presided over the rise of extremism has worked with every Pakistani administration since my government was destabilized in 1996."

About the general elections in Pakistan, Mohtarma Benazir Bhutto said,

> *"My Party and I seek fair, free and impartial elections to be held by an independent election commission under an interim government of national consensus. They want a level playing field for all candidates and parties. The Musharraf Election Commission has failed to give civil society and the opposition confidence."*

Regarding her return home from exile, she said, "I chose Karachi as the city to return to because it is the city where the founder of Pakistan rests. Quaid-e-Azam Mohammad Ali Jinnah campaigned to create Pakistan as a democracy where all citizens would be equal irrespective of their race, their religion or their gender. I go to Karachi to rekindle the dream of Quaid-e-Azam for the people of Pakistan. My father gave his life standing up for Quaid-e-Azam's dream of Pakistan. And so Karachi is full of symbolism for me. I do not know what awaits me, personally or politically, once I leave the airport. I pray for the best and prepare for the worst. But in any case, I am going home to fight for the restoration of Pakistan's place in the community of democratic nations. I do not fear the extremists for I have put my fate in the hands of the people of Pakistan, and my faith in God."

When I Return To Pakistan

Benazir Bhutto

I am returning to Pakistan on October 18, 2007 to bring change to my country. Pakistan's future viability, stability and security lie in empowering its people and building political institutions. My goal is to prove that the fundamental battle for the hearts and minds of a generation can be accomplished only under democracy.

The central issue facing Pakistan is moderation vs. extremism. The resolution of this issue will affect the world, particularly South and Central Asia and all Muslim nations.

Extremism can flourish only in an environment where basic governmental social responsibility for the welfare of the people is neglected. Political dictatorship and social hopelessness create the desperation that fuels religious extremism. Throughout Pakistan's 60-year history, weaving between dictatorship and democracy, from free elections to rigged elections to no elections, religious fundamentalists have never been a significant part of our political consciousness. They are inherently a centrist, moderate nation. Historically, the religious parties have not received more than 11 per cent of the vote in national elections. The largest political party is mine, the Pakistan People's Party (PPP). Pakistan's political landscape has been moulded primarily by the moderate PPP, which has demonstrated strong and continuous support from the rural masses and the urban elite. Extremism looms as a threat, but it will be contained as it has been in the past if the moderate middle can be mobilized to stand up to fanaticism. I return to lead that battle.

I have led an unusual life. I have buried a father killed at the age 50 and two brothers killed in the prime of their lives. I raised my children as a single mother when my husband was arrested and held for eight years without a conviction a hostage to my political career. I made my choice when the mantle of political leadership was thrust upon my shoulders after my father's murder. I did not shrink from responsibility then, and I will not shrink from it now.

Those who cast the vote decide nothing. Those who count the vote decide everything." That's why we have stressed electoral reforms although our efforts have so far been in vain. President Bush has rightly noted, "The most powerful weapon in the struggle against extremism is not bullets or bombs it is the universal appeal of freedom. Freedom is the design of our maker, and the longing of every soul." When my flight lands in Pakistan next month, I know I will be greeted with joy by the people. I do not know what awaits me, personally or politically, once I leave the airport. I pray for the best and prepare for the worst. But in any case, I am going home to fight for the restoration of Pakistan's place in the community of democratic nations.

New future for Pakistan

In a news item, published in The Observer, Benazir Bhutto, the former Prime Minister of Pakistan, vowed to go 'back to basics' and invoke her late father's name to win her way back into power in her country.

Bhutto, who was exiled from Pakistan eight years ago after two stints in government that both ended amid accusations of incompetence and scandal, said her campaign would be inspired by the old slogan of her Pakistan People's Party (PPP) - 'food, clothing, shelter'.

'Under my leadership, the PPP will bring moderation, democracy and the basics that the nation's poorest need,' she said. 'They represent the underprivileged, the peasants, women, young people, the minorities, all those who have been neglected by elite governments.'

Bhutto, many of whose key supporters are drawn from among the so-called 'feudal' landowners of Pakistan's south and east, confirmed talks with representatives of General Pervez Musharraf, who has ruled Pakistan since taking power in a bloodless coup in 1999. 'Pakistani politics is a rollercoaster ride,' Bhutto told The Observer. 'They were 80 per cent there, then negotiations stalled, then we started off again. My return will take place irrespective of the dialogue process.'

Bhutto, educated at Oxford and Harvard and the first woman to govern a post-colonial Muslim state, risks imprisonment if she returns to Pakistan, as multi-million-pound corruption charges dating from the mid-1990s are still pending. However, with his popularity at an all-time low, Musharraf may be tempted to do a constitutional deal with Bhutto to give his rule some much-needed domestic and international democratic legitimacy.

Time is, however, running out for the former premier to return. Both Bhutto and Nawaz Sharif, the Prime Minister ousted in a coup by Musharraf nine years ago and subsequently given a life sentence for hijacking, want to be present for presidential elections that, for constitutional reasons, have to be held within four months, but are likely to take place within six weeks.

Bhutto is now almost certain to return herself, albeit after Sharif. To become premier once more, she would have to reverse a constitutional amendment passed in the aftermath of the 1999 coup and directed at her and Sharif that limits individuals to two terms as Prime Minister. 'I am doing this for the constitution, not for personal benefit,' Bhutto said.

Bhutto insisted that her policies would bring growth, jobs and healthcare to Pakistan's poor. 'Food, clothing and shelter, that's the basis of the PPP,' said the veteran politician, who splits her time between Dubai and London. The slogan was coined by her father, Zulfiqar Ali Bhutto, when he launched the PPP in 1967, 12 years before he was hanged by military dictator Zia ul-Haq.

Despite a series of referendums and elections, Musharraf has never successfully established a strong democratic base and has been forced to rely on fringe groups or breakaway factions of Pakistan's main political parties to bolster his rule.

Critics say this has led to a surge in Islamic militancy; yesterday a bomb exploded outside an army-run bank in the restive frontier town of Peshawar. Musharraf has struggled to maintain a balance between policies that please Western allies such as the US and that are acceptable to a population that has shown itself to be increasingly anti-American. The recent armed assault on Islamic militants who had been allowed to establish a stronghold in a mosque in the centre of Islamabad, the capital, was well received by the West and endorsed by Bhutto, but caused angry demonstrations in much of Pakistan.

Pakistan's Moment of Truth

An article of Benazir Bhutto written for *Tribune Media Services, London.*

There are moments in history that prove decisive and mark a turning point for the future. The American Civil War was such a moment in the United States. The fall of the Berlin Wall was such a moment for Germany and the European Union. Today is Pakistan's moment of truth. Decisions made now will determine whether extremism and terrorism can be contained in Pakistan to save it from internal collapse. The stability of not just Pakistan but the civilized world is at stake.

In a democratic Pakistan, extremist movements have been minimal. In all democratic elections in my country, extremist religious parties have never garnered more than 11 per cent of the vote. Extremism under democracy has been marginalized by the people of Pakistan. But under dictatorship - most notably under military dictator General Muhammad Zia-ul-Haq in the 1980s but unfortunately also under General Pervez Musharraf during this decade - religious extremism has gained a foothold in my homeland.

Whether leaders like Zia manipulated and exploited religion for their own political ends, or whether dictatorship inherently induces deprivation, desperation and hopelessness, the fact remains that extremism has emerged as a threat to my nation, to the region and to the world. These extremists are the petri dish of international terrorism. It need not be so. It must be reversed. And it can be done.

In both of my tenures as prime minister, my government imposed the rule of law on all areas of Pakistan - our four provinces and also the federally administered tribal areas, including Waziristan. With the support of the people of those tribal areas, we managed to uproot an international drug cartel that had operated with impunity under dictatorship.

Today, however, the international drug barons have morphed into religious extremists and terrorists. The current government of Pakistan has ceded large areas of our nation to the pro-Taliban and Al Qaeda forces claiming that these areas are ungovernable. I believe they are governable and that a democratic government can prove better in restoring the authority of the state.

They must be realistic about the history and political reality of Pakistan. In a perfect world, perhaps the military would not play a role in politics. Pakistan is less than perfect in this regard. The security forces have fundamentally served as a political institution in Pakistan, ruling either directly through generals or indirectly by manipulating and ultimately sacking democratic governments.

I know that some people have been surprised that I have been negotiating a transition to democracy and talking about the future of Pakistan with Musharraf. They confront two great polarities in Pakistan today—the battle between democracy and dictatorship, and the fight for the hearts and souls of the people manifest in the battle between moderation and extremism.

On dictatorship, there can be no compromise. The Parliament must be supreme. I have signaled to Musharraf that the Pakistan People's Party supports the Constitution of Pakistan, which prevents a military president, and requires that a civilian president be legitimately selected by the parliament and provincial assemblies of the country.

The military ban on twice-elected prime ministers holding office again was not part of Pakistan's Constitution nor that of other parliamentary democracies and must be abolished. There must be immunity granted to all members of parliament and public officials elected before the military coup of 1999 who have not been convicted of any offense from politically inspired charges. All parties and all party leaders must be allowed to freely contest elections. A neutral caretaker government, pursuant to our constitution, must be empowered to oversee the nation before the elections, and a neutral and independent election commission, with the participation of all political parties, must be constituted.

Election rolls must be free from political manipulation. Balloting must be transparent, counting must be free from political intervention, and the entire process must be monitored by international observers to insure its sanctity and validity.

But free and fair elections alone are not enough to solve the problems of Pakistan. They must have free, fair and effective governing. And that requires that all responsible, moderate forces are mobilized, working for the same plan.

Musharraf continues to enjoy the support of the international community and the armed forces of Pakistan. But such support is no substitute for the will of the people who are disempowered and disenchanted. Growing poverty and unemployment make it clear that in the absence of democracy, the people's needs cannot be met. I believe that unless the people of Pakistan are empowered through the ballot, extremists will continue to exploit the discontent to their advantage.

The political madrassas are able to offer monthly stipends, food and clothing to families of the underprivileged. Unless government can move in to fill the vacuum, extremists will continue to exploit the situation, expanding their influence through the country.

I believe that moderation cannot be compromised and that democracy and moderation go together. Like many Pakistanis, I am pained that part of our land in the tribal areas has been ceded to terrorists.

Some argue that through ceasefires and peace treaties, one can get the extremists into the mainstream and moderate them. But the experience in Pakistan proves otherwise. Every ceasefire and peace treaty has emboldened the militants and terrorists. Nowhere was this more profoundly demonstrated than during the siege of the Red Mosque in Islamabad this summer.

Militants holed up in the political madrassa mutinied and tried to impose their own laws over and above the laws of the Constitution. They kidnapped women and police officials. They intimidated and shut down entertainment shops. Six long months of negotiations failed and a bloody result ensued when the army tried to overcome the mutiny. There were over 100 casualties.

The Red Mosque incident demonstrated that no deals can be struck with religious fanatics. They will attempt to run our country like they run the political madrassas. That is unacceptable. The militants must know that the Constitution and laws of Pakistan do not permit for private militias enforcing private laws in violation of the constitution of the country. There must be a coalescence of moderation to confront the extremist. Such a coalition can come from the expression of the free will of the people. That is the government and the kind of national movement that I believe we can lead.

Pakistan is at the crossroads. Their success can be a signal to 1 billion Muslims all over the world that Islam, which emphasizes the importance of consultation, is compatible with democracy, modernity and moderation. I go back to Pakistan this autumn knowing that there will be difficult days ahead. But I put my faith in the people and my fate in the hands of God. I am not afraid. Yes, we are at a turning point, but I know that time, justice and the forces of history are on our side.

Conversation with Benazir Bhutto

Gen. Pervez Musharraf may sense that his days as President of Pakistan could be numbered. So he has been talking to his former archrival, Benazir Bhutto, about a possible power-sharing arrangement. Bhutto, who was twice prime minister of Pakistan and is currently leader of the popular opposition party PPP, is on the verge of deciding whether to strike a deal with Musharraf or join the opposition against him. She sat down with Newsweek-Washington Post's Lally Weymouth in New York to talk about her options. Excerpts:

Q. Some say that if you make a deal with President Musharraf to return to power, it will diminish your popularity.

A. Many in my party have been urging me to distance myself from General Musharraf. They say his popularity ratings are down. But I am trying to convince them that the international community and the armed forces have confidence in Musharraf, and therefore we need to work out a solution [with him]. Their goal is to strengthen the forces of moderation and that's why we've been involved in this negotiation with General Musharraf.

Now we are at a critical point where I am being tugged in two directions — between those in the party who believe in dialogue and those who think that time is running out and that we can't spend more time talking unless there are upfront confidence-building measures.

Q. What have you asked President Musharraf to do?

A. They want a balance of power, reforms for a fair election, lifting of the ban on a twice-elected prime minister [running for a third term], as well as immunity for all holders of public office prior to 1999 or 2000. Where there are unproven charges that go back now for more than a decade or two, a chapter should be closed. General Musharraf has told me he wants this.

Q. Did you tell Musharraf that he would have to step down as army chief of staff if you entered into partnership with him?

A. I told him that we could not have a working arrangement with the army chief of staff. His term finishes either this November or December, so we are concerned that there should not be an extension on that.

Q. What did he say?

A. He has said that he would respect the constitution. Even if the president is not the army chief of staff, he would still appoint the heads of the military, so he would still control the military as the commander-in-chief.

Q. What are the other issues that stand between you and him?

A. One issue is the power of the President to sack the Parliament. This power was used in the '90s to destabilize democracy, so we are saying it must go

Q. The presidents kept dismissing governments?

A. Yes, we believe this was actually done at the request of the security services. The political parties were discredited and the militants grew in strength. But we feel that having 10 governments in 10 years leads to a collapse in governance. The extremists benefit from the chaos.

Q. Is that what stands between you, Musharraf and a deal?

A. That's one issue, but what stands between us right now is confidence-building steps which were promised and which we want done by the end of the month.

Q. Such as?

A. Lifting the ban on a twice-elected prime minister. He said yes to that in July. And also immunity to holders of public office from 1988 to 2000. He said yes to that in January of this year.

Q. So Musharraf hasn't lifted the ban on your serving a third term?

A. I expected him to do the lifting of the ban on the twice-elected prime minister and the immunity for public officers by the end of August. Because he plans to get elected 15 days later in September. So my party needs to see these steps if we are expected to take a certain course of action during the elections.

Q. In other words, if you are expected to support him?

A. He doesn't want our support, but he doesn't want us going out on the streets and agitating against him. My party says that we have to oppose the presidential election because it is illegal. I have said that if he takes confidence-building measures, then we don't have to vote for him but we don't have to create a ruckus in the streets.

Q. Can Musharraf get elected without your party?

A. Yes. He told me, 'I don't want your vote.' I advised him that it was better not to seek election from this assembly but to seek election from the next assembly because he would have greater legitimacy without a uniform, elected by a democratic verdict. But he has a different perspective. He thinks it is legal to be elected by this assembly. So we have left it to the courts to decide.

Q. The courts might rule against him?

A. I think the courts will rule it is illegal.

Q. Then what?

A. If he does not want us to resign now and join an opposition movement, he needs to take measures.

Q. What do you say to critics who say you cannot control the army?

A. I say that I controlled the army better than any of the others. When I was prime minister, the tribal areas were part of Pakistan. Now their control has been ceded to the militants and pro-Taliban forces. I did not allow a situation to develop with India that could lead to a war like the one that took place under [former prime minister] Nawaz Sharif. I could not stop the intelligence from destabilizing my government, because I didn't have the presidential power to appoint the service chiefs. When I was prime minister, I worked closely with the military to get an agreement on no export of nuclear technology. It was subsequently violated we don't know whether it was an individual act or because of one of the governments that came and went. I could not stop them from some actions of which I did not approve and for which they got clandestine presidential approval.

Q. If your deal materializes, Musharraf will control the army?

A. Yes, and I don't want the security services to disagree with my attack on internal militancy and get him to sack the Parliament once again. I'd be setting myself up to repeat the past. Which is why President must give up the power [to dissolve the Parliament]. In a perfect situation, the prime minister should have power over the armed services. But in this transition period, if Musharraf is still commander-in-chief of the armed forces, he will still appoint the army chiefs.

Q. Have you heard from him lately?

A. Yes. He's getting back to me by the end of the month. He has to decide. The people who are stopping him are Chaudhry Shujaat [president of the Pakistan Muslim League, Pakistan's ruling party]. He is telling Musharraf to go with the enemy the religious parties [known as the MMA] and we can get you reelected and we don't need the PPP. I think Chaudhry Shujaat is setting Musharraf up for failure. He's saying, 'Seek election and I will be your cover candidate.' A lot of the people involved in the Afghan jihad are with him. If Musharraf is knocked out by the courts, guess who will be the president? Chaudhry Shujaat. It's under his party that the extremists have spread in power. Musharraf thinks he needs these people but they are planning to depose him. He trusts them because he's been working with them. To us, it's a fight between moderation and extremism.

Q. Do you think Musharraf is a moderate?

A. He says he is a moderate, but if so, he has to strengthen the moderate forces.

Q. Can you make an alliance with Nawaz Sharif [head of the Pakistan Muslim League N, or Nawaz group]?

A. If our negotiations with Musharraf fall apart, we can always turn to the other political party. But Nawaz Sharif and I had a falling out over the MMA. I think they are the supporters of extremist groups. Nawaz wanted an alliance with them and I did not. As long as he is with them and they are in government, we will go as a third force. The military tries to say that the alternative [to Musharraf] is the religious parties, which is not the right argument. The third force is the democratic force. Since 2002, the military and the religious parties and Shujaat have been in power. This alliance has ceded territory to the pro-Taliban forces in the tribal areas and ceded ground in our cities to the militants. And they neglected the people: Unemployment has risen. Musharraf has to decide whether to go with the moderate forces and to accept the people's democratic choice.

Q. Unless the United States pressures him, will he go that way?

A. He says he has an interest, but Chaudhry and those who supported the rise of militancy don't have an interest and are trying to sabotage the understanding.

Q. So will you return to Pakistan?

A. I'm planning to go back between September and December. I need to be there to strengthen my party and the moderate forces.

Q. Are you worried you will be arrested?

A. As things stand, it will be difficult to arrest me. There is a risk, but I am prepared to take it.

Q. Didn't Musharraf make a big mistake when he fired the chief justice?

A. Yes, it was a very big mistake.

Q. Who was behind it?

A. I think he received wrong information that the action was legal and would be upheld by the courts. People who wanted to weaken him did that.

The fact that Musharraf has extended his term as army chief so many times has not gone down well with the armed forces. There's public discontent over the involvement of the army in the running of the state.

Q. How did you keep going all these years in exile?

A. The people of my country supported me and the Pakistani community encouraged me. So did my husband and my children. My husband was in prison for eight years and he never once told me he could not take it anymore. My children never told me not to travel.

A Conversation With Benazir Bhutto

Presider: Richard N. Haass, President, Council on Foreign Relations

RICHARD N. HAASS: Good afternoon and welcome to a special meeting of the Council on Foreign Relations. It's special because it's August — (laughter) — and we try not to do too many meetings in August. It's also special because of the subject and our speaker here today, the former prime minister of Pakistan .

Their timing is good. This week marks the 60th anniversary of Pakistan . And our timing is good for another reason, which is, Pakistan has been, is and, I would predict, will be much in the news for days, weeks, months and longer to come.

It's hard to imagine someone better placed to speak about the current situation in Pakistan than Benazir Bhutto. She was born into one of Pakistan 's leading political families. She was educated at both Harvard and Oxford. And — full confession — let me say that she and I met some — at the risk of being less than gallant — 30 years ago or so at Oxford. They would have met even earlier than that, at Harvard, except she got accepted and I did not. (Laughter.) And of such things history is made. (Laughter.) I'm almost over it, by the way. (Laughter.)

And Benazir Bhutto has twice been prime minister of her country, from 1988 to 1990, as well as from 1993 to 1996. And now and before, her fans and her critics alike, I believe, would agree that she has been an important — indeed, critical — voice in that country's trajectory, regardless of her physical location. It's been a number of years — a year or so?

BENAZIR BHUTTO: Eight years.

HAASS: — eight years since she's been able to be in her country. And I expect one of the things we will talk about is when that situation is likely to change.

The way we are going to do it today is, Ms. Bhutto will speak for about 10 minutes. You will hear her voice. Then you will hear for a few minutes our voices, and then we will reserve the bulk of the time this afternoon to hear your voice, any comments or, more likely, questions you have.

They've also already begun collecting questions from our national members who are wired into this event by the wonders of modern technology.

As you no doubt notice, because you are here, we started approximately 30 minutes earlier than we normally start. And in the political or institutional equivalent of the theory of the conservation of time, we will end 30 minutes earlier than usual, so those of you catching the Jitney to the Hamptons will not be delayed.

It is, for me, a personal pleasure to welcome back to the Council on Foreign Relations an old friend of mine and someone who is familiar to many of you in this room and knows well this organization, the former prime minister of Pakistan, Benazir Bhutto.

BHUTTO: Thank you.

Ladies and gentlemen, it's a privilege for me to be here this afternoon as the guest of the Council on Foreign Relations. Thank you for inviting me.

And as I come here to have a conversation with you, I find that my country, Pakistan, is once again in a crisis, and it's a crisis that threatens not only my nation and region, but possible could have repercussions on the entire world.

It's a crisis that has its roots almost half a century ago, when the military in my country first seized power, in 1958. Four military dictatorships and most recently those of General Zia ul-Haq in the '80s and now General Musharraf have ruled my nation for the last 30 years, except for a few years of civilian government. And so I believe that democracy has never really been given a chance to grow or nurture in my homeland.

As an example, I was only allowed to govern for five of the 10 years that my people elected me to govern. And now Pakistan has changed dramatically from the days when I left office, in 1996, for now, from areas previously controlled by my government, pro-Taliban forces linked to al Qaeda launch regular attacks on NATO troops across the border in Afghanistan.

In the view of my party, military dictatorship, first in the '80s and now again, under General Musharraf, has fueled the forces of extremism, and military dictatorship puts into place a government that is unaccountable, that is unrepresentative, undemocratic, and disconnected from the ordinary people in the country, disconnected from the aspirations of the people who make up Pakistan. Moreover, military dictatorship is born from the power of the gun, and so it undermines the concept of the rule of law and gives birth to a culture of might, a culture of weapons, violence and intolerance.

The suppression of democracy in my homeland has had profound institutional consequences. The major infrastructure building blocks of democracy have been weakened, political parties have been marginalized, NGOs are dismantled, judges sacked and civil society undermined. And by undermining the infrastructure of democracy, the regime that is in place to date was a regime put into place by the intelligence agencies after the flawed elections of 2002. This regime has not allowed the freedom of association, the freedom of movement, the freedom of speech for moderate political forces, and so by default, the mosques and the madrassas have become the only outlet of permitted political expression in the country.

And so just as the we've seen the emergence of the religious parties, we've seen the emergence of the extremist groups, and just as the military dictatorship of the '80s used the so-called Islamic card to promote a military dictatorship while demonizing political parties, so too the present military establishment of this century has used the so-called Islamist card to pressurize the international community into supporting military dictatorship once again.

But I am here this afternoon to tell you that as far as we, the Pakistan People's Party, is concerned, the choice in Pakistan is not really between military dictatorship and religious parties; the choice for Pakistan is indeed between dictatorship and democracy. And I feel that the real choice that the world also faces today is the choice between dictatorship and democracy, and in the choice that we make between dictatorship and democracy lies the outcome of the battle between extremism and moderation in Pakistan.

The U.S. intelligence recent threat assessment stated that, and I quote, "Al Qaeda and the Taliban seem to be fairly well-settled into the safe haven spaces of Pakistan. They see more training, we see more money, we see more communications, we see that activity rising." That's the most recent U.S. national intelligence threat assessment. And so it's often surprising to those of us in Pakistan who see the international community back the present regime. But this backing continues, despite the regime's failure to stop the Taliban and al Qaeda reorganizing after they were defeated, demoralized and dispersed following the events of 9/11.

This is a regime under which the religious parties have risen, for the first time, to power, and they run two of Pakistan's four federating units two most critical states of Pakistan, those that border Afghanistan. And even while the military dictatorship has allowed the religious parties to govern two of Pakistan 's most critical four provinces, it has exiled the moderate leadership of the country, it has weakened internal law enforcement and allowed for a very bloody suppression of people's human rights.

The military operation in Baluchistan is an example of the brutality of the suppression. The killings that took place in Karachi on May 12th, where 48 peaceful political activists were gunned down in the streets of Karachi, and not one person has been arrested for those murders that were actually televised, shows the level to which the regime permits the suppression of the political opposition. And most recently, 17 members of my party were killed in Islamabad on July 17 at the hands of a suicide bomber.

The weakness of law enforcement has led to a series of suicide bombings, roadside bombings. To give you an example, since last July, 300 people have fallen victim to suicide bombers within Pakistan. Disappearances, too, which were unheard of in our country's history, have become the order of the day. And even as I speak to you, a Pak-origin American, Dr. Sarki, has disappeared, not because he supports extremists, but because he's a nationalist, and the level of intolerance for differing views is so high that people can disappear simply for supporting nationalism.

The West's close association with a military dictatorship, in my humble view, is alienating Pakistan's people and is playing into the hands of those hardliners who blame the West for the ills of the region. And it need not be this way. A people inspired by democracy, human rights and economic opportunity will turn their back decisively against extremism.

There is a silver lining on the clouds. The recent restoration of the chief justice of Pakistan to the Supreme

Court has given hope to people of Pakistan that the unchecked power of the military will now finally come under a degree of scrutiny by the highest judicial institutions in the country. They in the PPP have kept the doors of dialogue open with the military regime to facilitate the transfer of democracy. This hasn't been a popular move, but we've done it because we think the stability of Pakistan is important to our own security as well as to regional security.

However, without progress on the issue of fair elections, this dialogue could founder. And now, as we approach the autumn, time is running out.

Ladies and gentlemen, I plan to return later this year to Pakistan to lead a democratic movement for the restoration of democracy. I seek to lead a democratic Pakistan which is free from the yoke of military dictatorship and that will cease to be a haven, the very petri dish of international terrorism. A democratic Pakistan that would help stabilize Afghanistan, relieving pressure on NATO troops. A democratic Pakistan that would pursue the drug barons and bust up the drug cartel that today is funding terrorism. A Pakistan where the rule of law is established so that no one has the permission to establish, recruit, train and run private armies and private militias. A democratic Pakistan that puts the welfare of its people as the centerpiece of its national policy.

And as I plan to return to Pakistan, I put my faith in the people of my country who have stood by my party and by myself through this long decade more than a decade, 11 years since the PPP government was ousted because they believe that the PPP can eliminate terrorism and give them security, and security will bring in the economic investment that can help us reverse the tide of rising poverty in the country, and by so doing, it will certainly undermine the forces of militancy and extremism.

I thank you all for listening to me so patiently.

HAASS: Well, thank you.

And before I ask a few questions, just to remind people, if they haven't shut off their cell phones or their Black Berrys, please do. And this is obviously on the record. And as I said, there are people listening in around the country and around the world who are our national members.

You talk about the history of your country over the last 60 years. What is it about Pakistan or Pakistanis that accounts for the fact that, probably a majority of its history, democracy has not prevailed. What's wrong?

BHUTTO: Well, we feel that the founder of Pakistan, Quaid-e-Azam Mohammed Ali Jinnah, died very quickly, a year after Pakistan was founded, and so we didn't have a national leader with the authority, the respect to help us develop our democratic political institutions, whereas Nehru, in nearby India, provided the leadership that could help a new nation strengthen its democratic institutions.

Secondly, we also feel that Pakistan's geostrategic position as a country you know, Afghanistan was the buffer state during the Cold War, and Pakistan was one side of the buffer state so our geostrategic position as the bastion for the free world also led to the international community dealing with whoever was in power. So in a sense, the military dictatorships were able to milk international support for suppressing democratic rights for short-term strategic goals. But I am concerned that that policy is now backfiring.

HAASS: Do you therefore actually wish that the United States and others were putting more pressure on your government to reinstall democracy?

BHUTTO: Yes, I would very much like to see the United States link its support, its financial and military assistance to Pakistan, to the restoration of democracy, to the holding of elections that are free, fair and impartial and open to all political parties. But for me, the restoration of democracy is only the first step. I would like to see the international community make a long-term commitment to a country as critical as Pakistan and indeed our nearby neighbour, Afghanistan, in helping us to build our institutions.

In 1988, when democracy was restored, the military establishment was still very powerful. The extremist groups were still there. And when the aid and assistance to Pakistan was cut, we had to adopt harsh economic policies. So in a way, it showed that democracy doesn't pay, and the military was able to reassert itself.

So I'd like to see a much longer-term commitment. Europe made a long-term commitment. When Europe was driven by war, the international community put NATO troops in Europe, and it made a long-term commitment through the Marshall Plan to develop the institutions. So I know it's unpopular, but I don't see quick fixes. I think what's needed is the restoration of democracy but also a commitment to help the institutions of a nation be built to sustain that democracy.

HAASS: If this is going to happen, two, if you will, constituencies in Pakistan are going to have to agree. One is the army. Do you think there is a consensus in the army to essentially return to the barracks?

BHUTTO: I doubt that there's a consensus. I don't get that sense. But I do get the sense that the army right now is itself uncomfortable with its role. The public has turned against the uniform General Musharraf as the uniform and there are reports that the military personnel have been told not to wear their uniforms when they go into the streets. So in that sense, the rank and file does not like being unpopular. It's used to being respected by the people at large. And so to make the army non controversial, it's important to get them out of the politics.

But there are a group within the armed forces who are the top leadership who have a vested interest in dictatorship, because dictatorship brings power not only to them, but it brings power to their relatives, who then start doing well in parliamentary elections which are rigged, or then start doing well economically because business contracts go that way. So that I feel that as far as the rank and file of the Pakistani army is concerned, they'd like to get out and they'd like to let the civilians do the job, but I'm not sure that's what the leadership feels.

HAASS: The other key constituency, if you will, is a rather fundamental one, which is the Pakistani people. And I suppose the question that comes to mind is whether you now have in Pakistan a significant chunk of the population how would I put it? that is more committed to its ideology than it is to institutions and democracy, that the process of radicalization and the rise of extremism in your country has now created a significant obstacle or hurdle to the restoration of democracy.

BHUTTO: I know that that's an argument that some of the supporters of the military regime say, that elections in Pakistan could give up a Hamas-type solution, but that's not what the polls show, that's not what the elections have shown. Since the inception of Pakistan, all the elections have shown that the religious parties never do well when it comes to elections.

And secondly, the most recent poll by the IRI, the International Republican Institute, also showed that the religious parties would not do well. So they cannot gain through a fair, free and impartial election. However, if the military establishment decides rig the elections, that's another issue, which is why we in the PPP have asked General Musharraf to implement certain reforms to ensure that the elections will be fair, and we have also requested the international community to fund a robust monitoring team to ensure that those elections are fair.

HAASS: When you talk about your commitment to going back later this year, are there any preconditions that either you have set or have been set for you that you are at liberty to discuss?

BHUTTO: Well, General Musharraf would not like me to come. He has publicly stated that he would not like me and Mr. Nawaz Sharif to return before the end of the year. He says it will be destabilizing if Mr. Nawaz Sharif and I return to lead our parties in the election campaign. Both of us don't agree because we feel our return will be destabilizing to the ruling party known as the Muslim League-Q, but it won't be destabilizing to the nation, it won't be destabilizing necessarily to the presidency. And we feel that elections cannot be free and fair unless the leaders of all parties are allowed to contest and contest freely.

I mean what sort of an election would we have, for example, in America if, in a presidential contest Rudy Giuliani was allowed to campaign and Hillary Clinton wasn't? It would give an unfair advantage to one side.

HAASS: But implicit in the we won't go there.

Implicit in what I hear you saying is General or President Musharraf 's desire to essentially get this round of elections out of the way before you and Mr. Sharif or both of you were to return, and I don't know whether implicit in that is that he's essentially saying, okay, next time to participate, but not this time.

BHUTTO: That's what he said the last time (laughter) but the issue is that what are the choices before General Musharraf? Last time he had a choice to keep the two of us out, and he had the choice to put together a political party that he said would address the social needs of the people and contain terrorism.

Secondly, the choice before him today is not between allowing us back afterwards, the choice is either facilitating a transfer to democracy to keep Pakistan stable and to try and broker an arrangement where he will also be continuing; or alternatively, to have all the political parties gang up against him where he could risk a movement in the streets that is stronger than the recent one which the lawyers waged.

So I don't think the options he has before him are the same as the last one, and I would rather seek to persuade him to permit an election, which will enhance his own reputation, that people could respect him for holding fair elections. But if there's a perception that the elections have been stolen, it could be like Ukraine and the Orange

Revolution, where the civil groups and the political parties get together and force him out.

HAASS: Could you imagine yourself to use the French concept entering into cohabitation with somebody such as President Musharraf?

BHUTTO: Well, it would depend on how the event unfolded. At the moment, the situation is this, but we have been having a negotiation for almost a year. And while there's been agreement on several issues and where General Musharraf has committed to taking certain confidence-building measures, those haven't been taken. So my party's asking that you know, is it just the talk or is it going to turn into a walk? So that would very much depend on what happens up front and whether we have an understanding.

They have tried to have it, and it's not easy because, you know, the IRI polls showed that two-thirds of Pakistanis feel he's very unpopular and should go. But we are risking our popularity by even having this dialogue, but we understand Pakistan is a critical country. They understand that instability in Pakistan could threaten our own security as well as that of the region, so we've taken the risk, but we really need General Musharraf also to come up with the measures that he has already promised, to implement the measures that he has already promised by the end of this month, preferably.

HAASS: Let me turn to we'll obviously have more questions on that, but let me turn, if I may, for a moment to some questions about Pakistan's relationship with its neighbours and with others.

It's almost a year now since the so-called Miranshah am I pronouncing it right? agreement, which essentially was a special arrangement, we'll call it, between the central government and North Waziristan .

And quite honestly in this country and elsewhere, it's been widely criticized as constituting a form of appeasement, where the central government essentially allowed people far too much discretion, autonomy what have you to do what they would, including getting involved in ways, across the border with Afghanistan, including conceivably ways of supporting al Qaeda. What is your stance about what should be done in terms of dealing with North Waziristan and more generally with that part of the country?

BHUTTO: Well, Pakistan People's Party and I rejected that ceasefire of September 2006 — the peace treaty and we rejected the ceasefires before that. In fact, we were appalled that the tribal region of our country was handed over to foreigners, because Afghan Taliban, Afghans and al Qaeda are added to the Chechens and the Uzbeks. And this is Pakistani territory, and Pakistan has to protect its own territory.

So we've been absolutely appalled by that. And we think the first thing the government of Pakistan has to do is to take the territory back. They've ceded authority of our own territory, and it's not enough to satisfy the agenda of the Afghan Taliban or the Arab al Qaeda or the Central Asian Uzbek-Chechen. They're now knocking on the doors of our frontier province.

There's been an attempt to take over the city of Darra Adam Khel. They've tried to take over Tank; they've tried to take over Malakand. The more you give them; the more they want.

HAASS: What about the argument the other way? When people make your point often in Washington, one hears the argument that if one pushed General Musharraf or President Musharraf to do just that, his own security forces be it elements of the army or elements of the ISI, the Intelligence Directorate would not prove loyal, that essentially if he pushed things that far, he himself would be challenged. What do you say when you hear that kind of an argument?

BHUTTO: When I hear that argument, I hear two kinds of arguments. One of the arguments that I hear is that he's not going to push them too far, because then he'll be deposed. But the issue is that when you are the chief of army staff and you control basically all the bombs in Pakistan, then you've got to put together a team that will support you and give you the base that will corner the people who are the extremists so that you'll not topple. You've got to take them on. Because if you don't take them on, then they win the battle anyway. Whereas if you take them on, well, either you win and if you don't win, well, you've tried, and somebody is going to come in and try harder.

The second argument that I hear is that you've got to placate the hardliners. You've got to bring them into the mainstream and envigor the religious parties. You know, people tell me that Pakistan People's Party is so moderate that the people who are the militants and the extremists will get against it, and they won't let you work. But the issue is we won't let them work either.

Now what's happening is that we brought them into we've said, let's bring them into the mainstream. They've given them two provinces; we've given them the leader of opposition. And has it quenched their thirst? No, they want more and more. They want to take over the whole state of Pakistan, not on the basis of having the popular support but on the basis of having the support of the militants and the militias.

So this is a battle to save Pakistan. They have to save Pakistan from within. And by saving Pakistan from within, I think that it will be having a profound effect on our region. It will have an effect on Afghanistan, on India and also the larger world community.

Let's not forget that the Tube bomber in London happened to have visited my country, or that Abu Zubaydah or the CEO of al Qaeda — they were arrested from Pakistani cities. So the terrorists must know that Pakistan's not going to provide them an environment that they can visit safely. And I just need to understand why we have such a large intelligence if the intelligence is not able to intercept them. So my goal would be to put together a team that would give the support to the government to go after them relentlessly.

QUESTIONER: You may have covered that, what I was going to ask you next, but let me try it anyhow.

They had quite an interesting, and indeed still are, mini-debate here politically between two — initially two of the Democratic aspirants for presidents, and it spread now across party lines. And Barack Obama kicked it off by saying, "If we have actionable intelligence about high-value terrorist targets and President Musharraf won't act, we will." That's a direct quote from a recent speech of his. What is your reaction to that?

BHUTTO: Well, I wouldn't like the United States to violate Pakistan's sovereignty with unauthorized military operations. But the issue that I would like to stress is that Barack Obama also said, if Pakistan won't act. And that's the critical issue, that the government has to act. And the government has to act to protect Pakistan's own serenity and integrity, its own respect, and to understand that if it creates a vacuum, then others aren't going to just twiddle their thumbs while militants freely move across the border.

I think General Musharraf did the right thing recently in admitting that militants are using our soil, but he said the army has nothing to do with it. But nonetheless, the issue for me is that we cannot cede parts of Pakistani territory to anybody; not just the Taliban, to anybody. That in Pakistan we have one army, one police, one constitution, one government. They cannot allow parallel armies, parallel militias, parallel laws and parallel command structures. Today it's not just the intelligence services, who were previously called a state within a state. Today it's the militants who are becoming yet another little state within the state, and this is leading some people to say that Pakistan is on the slippery slope of being called a failed state. But this is a crisis for Pakistan, that unless we deal with the extremists and the terrorists, our entire state could founder.

HAASS: A sobering moment on which to open things up. So let me open it up to you all, our members. Wait for a microphone. Please state your name and your affiliation. And please limit yourself to one question so we can conceivably get lots of people in there.

Minky?

QUESTIONER: Minky Worden from Human Rights Watch. Welcome to New York.

Back to Richard's point about the possibility of an alliance with General Musharraf. In view of how he took power, wouldn't an alliance with him send the negative message to future coup plotters that elected politicians could legitimize them in the end?

BHUTTO: Yes, at one level it would send a negative message. But Pakistan isn't an ordinary country and it's not facing an ordinary situation now. They have two different faultlines. They have one faultline between dictatorship and democracy, and we have a second faultline between the forces of moderation and the forces of extremism. They have problems with General Musharraf because he's a coup leader, and dealing with him we have severe problems at that level.

But on the other hand, General Musharraf says and has committed himself to Pakistan following a moderate path. So to that extent, if he could get the moderate forces to work together for a transition to democracy, I think in the present circumstances it would be helpful. At least that's the decision my party took, and that's why we have been involved in these negotiations.

Whether it will work, frankly, I can't say. Time, as I said, is running out. General Musharraf made certain commitments to us and we would need to see the fulfillment of those commitments in the next two to three weeks before my party meets to take a final decision on where we stand.

HAASS: Rabbi Schneier? You have to wait for a microphone. That's how we do it in our synagogue here. (Laughter.)

QUESTIONER: You attributed the rise of the fundamentalism and radical extremism to the dictatorship and lack of democracy. The question: What would you do, and your party, to deal with the network of madrassas that are infiltrated with Wahhabi ideology? And we're not only talking about today. You're training an entire generation of children who do not believe in democracy. What will you do with it?

BHUTTO: Well, I agree with you that this is another very big challenge, because nowadays we have three kinds of madrassas in Pakistan. One is the traditional madrassa which teaches people their religious duties and obligations. The second is a madrassa which basically brainwashes our children into intolerance. The third madrassa is the one which is acting as the headquarters of the militant groups, as we saw in the issue of the Red Mosque.

I thank you for drawing my attention to the middle madrassa, which is the value system, because this is a battle for values, that are we going to move in the direction of a pluralistic society or not. And I feel that nobody in my country should have the right to teach people hate, to teach them violence and to brainwash them from the very beginning in extremist thought to prepare them, which is why we would like to reform those madrassas. And if anybody does not each the approved curriculum — or we don't even care about approved curriculums; what we care about is that you cannot teach people hate and you cannot teach them violence. You cannot say you have to kill people of a different faith or you have to kill people of a different ethnicity. So as long as madrassas abide by those rules, they will be allowed to function, and if they don't, they will be shut down.

HAASS: You don't feel, though, they should also have the responsibility to teach, say, the basics of science, math, whatever, so people can essentially function in a modern society and world?

BHUTTO: You know, Richard, it was in we did that, I did that. I know we talked about Musharraf now, but my government actually, everybody thinks the war on terrorism began now; for me, it began much earlier with the first attack on the World Trade Towers. And in 1993, Pakistan was on the brink of being declared a terrorist state. My government arrested Ramzi Yousef, the man who was behind the first attack on the World Trade Towers. My security people didn't want to give him up, because he had not only attacked the World Trade Towers, he had tried to kill me to stop me from becoming prime minister of Pakistan.

But I handed him over, and we began an investigation, and that's when we discovered these madrassas, political madrassas that had been set up secretly by (funds ?) during the Afghan jihad, and we found that there were students from 126 different countries who had come to be recruited and enrolled in these madrassas. And that's when my Ministry of Interior and my Ministry of Education worked together to introduce math and science into the madrassas. But we also said that you cannot teach hate, because it's not enough to teach them computers and science if they're still taught to discriminate on the basis of ethnicity and discriminate on the basis of religion. So we did all that.

What we found is as soon as our government went, they diverted to their own ways. So obviously we've got to stop them from teaching hate, and we've got to make them teach science and math and so on, but at the same time, a government in Pakistan has to commit to building schools not only building schools which people can go to, but building them on the mantra of madrassas, because the madrassas don't only give education; they give free food and clothing. So parents who are poor bring their children to the madrassas to be fed and looked after during the week. So my government had come up with a concept called Apna Ghar Your House where the government would set up boarding schools for people who are poor, and they could bring their children for free education and food and clothing.

Unless we provide an alternative to the madrassa it's not enough just trying to shut one down or reform the curriculum, so I think a multifaceted approach needs to be adopted.

HAASS: One of our members, Ricardo Tavares (sp), from Rancho Santa Fe, California, writes in and notes that the Pakistani economy has grown an average of 7 per cent a year over the last five years, and he talks about the important role that foreign direct investment has played. And the question I have is, based on his question, really, is if you were back in power, how much would your economic policies look like Shaukat Aziz's, the current prime minister? And how much would you be introducing changes from what we now see in Pakistan?

BHUTTO: Well, I want to put this in a different frame.

HAASS: Okay.

BHUTTO: And I want to say that I find the 7 per cent growth rate very disappointing, given the fact that all our loans have been rescheduled and given the fact that we are receiving $10 billion in overt and covert assistance. Because when I was prime minister of Pakistan, I left office while I had to pay off the debts and without all this money, with a 6 per cent growth rate, which started to go up in the year '96-'97 to 8 per cent. So I think Pakistan has a huge potential and that the present regime has got a 7 per cent growth rate more because of the debts being rescheduled and external flows coming in and not because of direct foreign investment.

There has been privatization. There have been a couple of groups from the Gulf that have come in, but name me one major international company, for example, like from America or from England I could name you General Electric, AES, National Power, who were all coming in when I was prime minister of Pakistan. But when you have terrorism and extremism and you have suicide bombers who are going and blowing up marketplaces and blowing up diplomatic missions and churches and (mosques ?) and places of worship, you don't get foreign investment. So we have a jobless recovery in Pakistan.

On paper, the statistics look good because you've got the external flows coming in. But in fact, poverty and unemployment in Pakistan has risen, and it's ticking like a time bomb. Because the people are unemployed and unemployment has risen, these militias and militants go to our people and say, we will give you a salary, we will pay you $150 or $200 a month; come and join our army.

So it's not just people who are ideologues who are joining the militants; it's jobless people who are being recruited in private armies. So, yes, I'm happy that flows are coming in and the debts are rescheduled and we've got 7 per cent. At one level I'm happy, but on another level I'm not, because I think that we need an economy which invites the investment, that produces the jobs and a government that addresses the social and economic needs of the people so they cannot be exploited by those who are criminals and terrorists.

HAASS: Yes, sir. I don't have my glasses on, so I can't see that far.

QUESTIONER: (Name and affiliation inaudible.) Madame Prime Minister, if you were elected and if you had been the authority to work with the world community on issues of terrorism, would it be easier or more difficult for you than it has been for Musharraf? I understand that it was a difficult decision for Musharraf to come in support of the United States and the alliance, the coalition of the willing.

BHUTTO: I want to tell you that there's a broad consensus in Pakistan between the major political parties that General Musharraf took the right step and that we have to fight terrorism. Mr. Nawaz Sharif and I have had our differences in the past, but we've come together and we've signed a Charter of Democracy. And in that both our parties were the major parties in Pakistan have committed to fighting terrorism and extremism. But while it may have been a difficult decision for Musharraf at one level, there is a consensus within Pakistan that terrorism is a threat to the outside world and it's also a threat to the people of Pakistan.

They want to work together with the international community to eliminate terrorism and extremism from our country. Would it be easier for us? Well, you know, this is a very interesting question. In some ways it would be easier for us, and in other ways it's easier for Musharraf. Musharraf's strong point is that he's got the army. Musharraf's strong point is he's got the intelligence. But at the same time, his difficulty is that this the same military security apparatus that fought the Afghan jihad of the '80s, that established the Afghan mujaheddin, who later went on to become the Taliban and al Qaeda.

So people who work together have certain social occasions together and find it more difficult to suddenly take on the people they were breaking bread with; whereas with us, while we certainly need the army in back-up situations and we certainly need the military intelligence, we have a different information. They have an information based on our public and our people and our support. They have the law enforcement in terms of police. They have paramilitary forces. So we can go directly to the people.

For instance, I was talking to one of my party people now when we were distributing tickets in England before coming here, and I said, how are you going to fight with these suicide bombers? And he said, well, if anybody tried to kill me in my area, my family would know immediately who it was because we know who's living in the next house, we know who's living in the next lane, and we wouldn't leave them we'd make sure that they were caught so they wouldn't dare to touch me. So having that kind of political or public information is very important.

The military establishment moves against all people. It doesn't identify the people who could be the troublemakers. So if our army is sent into the tribal areas, it's difficult for the army to assess when to bulldoze a home. Is that an extremist home or is that one which belongs to a member of the community? The equation changes, which is why our military did not have success in putting out the insurgency in Karachi in the '90s, but my government was able to do it. It wasn't easy; it took us a year, 15 months, but we did it because people from the public would come to us, to our elected representatives and meet with us and say, you know, it's that person and it's that person you should be watching. So we would get information from the public.

Because when the public are involved with the government and when the public are benefiting from a government in terms of jobs and schools and drinking water, the public want to save their own community. But when there is a government that is non-representative, the public becomes alienated, and the public are against the government. And it doesn't really make that much of a difference to the public whether it's, you know, Musharraf or whether it's the militants or whether it's the military. It only makes an effect when there's actually a suicide bombing in a particular locality.

So in some ways, a democratic government is stronger because it can reach the people and it can pull together the law enforcement; terrorism is as much a military situation as it is an investigative criminal situation. So I think what's needed is meshing together. Of course, if I had General Musharraf 's powers I mean, you know, powers over the military, powers over the police, powers over the seven administrations I think that this situation could be is not easily tackled, but could be tackled. They have state capacity and resources to tackle it. But the present regime has not been able to tackle it.

I know this answer is long. Bear with me for one minute more.

Law enforcement got hold of a chief cleric smuggling weapons into Islamabad. But was that police officer rewarded? No, he wasn't, because the cabinet minister intervened and freed the militant who was smuggling weapons into Islamabad.

So we cannot resolve the situation when law enforcement itself is demoralized for doing the job that it ought to be doing.

HAASS: As you raise legal issues, at the risk of being an ungracious host — you've been prime minister twice, obviously, and twice you've been dismissed, by two different presidents. Among the charges were obviously corruption. How do you deal with those charges?

BHUTTO: Well, I say that a person is innocent unless proved otherwise. And I say the very fact that I faced a state-sponsored persecution for 10 long years, which could have broken many other person(s) it's easy to litigate, go and have an investigation, and you go from city to city and country to country and continent to continent and courtroom to courtroom. But I was strong in my convictions. I defended myself. There's nothing against me. And my people also believe that a person is innocent unless proved otherwise.

However, I feel that this demonization process was taken to discredit the political class, divert attention from the institutionalized corruption of the military.

I wasn't the only prime minister who was sacked for corruption. Twice Mr. Nawaz Sharif was sacked for corruption. His predecessor Mr. Junejo was sacked for corruption. The prime minister of the '50s was sacked for corruption. And when the chief justice started showing too much independence, he was charged with corruption. When Mr. Imran Khan, the cricketer, who has one parliamentary seat, started defying the government, his wife was charged with smuggling tiles.

So these charges are concocted to put the political class on the defensive. This doesn't mean there isn't corruption. I think we do need to tackle corruption. I think we need transparency, we need a free press, and we need vibrant civil groups that act as watchdogs on government.

HAASS: Rita Hauser.

QUESTIONER: Hi. With some degree

HAASS: Please, wait for a microphone.

QUESTIONER: Sorry. Rita Hauser. With some degree of frequency we read, at least in the European press, about Sunni and Shi'a conflict, particularly in Karachi — one group attacking the mosques of the other, and some degree of violence in private militias. Is the Sunni-Shi'a divide an issue in Pakistan? And if so, what dimension?

BHUTTO: Well, unfortunately, intolerance is becoming an issue in Pakistan . It wasn't in the past. But while people are aware that these militant groups preach hatred against other religions for example, they say, "Kill the Christians, kill the Jews, kill the Hindus" most people are not aware that these extremist groups also preach hatred against different schools of Islam with different interpretations. So they also say, "Kill the Shi'as because they are non-believers." They also say fathers should kill their daughters if the daughters marry against the father's wishes.

So this issue is one of a dialogue between the Islamic world and the non-Islamic. But there's also a dialogue that is necessary within the Islamic world.

When I was growing up as a child, we were always taught that you shall have your religion, and I shall have my religion; that every religious group has to respect another religious interpretation, whether it is within the Muslim fold or outside.

But unfortunately, that's no longer the case. Ever since the extremists started attacking those religious groups who did not conform to their religious interpretation within Islam, including the Shi'as, then they organized themselves to hit back at those groups. And it's very painful for me as a Muslim to see that the place of worship, the mosque in Islam, which should be a place of refuge, has now turned into one where people fight and there is bloodshed and where their militants are stocking arms. It's a very disturbing phenomena for the majority of the Muslim people of Pakistan.

But you quite right; this kind of extremist interpretation is leading to sectarian warfare not only in Pakistan you've been very wise to pinpoint it — it's leading elsewhere in the Muslim world, too.

HAASS: There's about 40 or 50 people who have their hands up. So let me apologize for making 40 or 50 more enemies today. I'm off to an early start in our year.

QUESTIONER: Thank you. James Tunkey, I-OnAsia. Prime Minister, I would ask if you would request or recommend any changes to the U.S. military or intelligence or other types of aid or support in Pakistan.

BHUTTO: Well, I would like to see the U.S. military and economic aid to Pakistan continue. I think there needs to be a long-term commitment to security in the region. I sometimes hear — I mean, in this tribal jirga, for example, that was held, some people said the way to restore peace is to withdraw NATO from Afghanistan. I don't agree. I think it takes a generation to build up different attitudes, different beliefs different institutions. I remember Afghanistan being without any institution at all.

So I think it's important to make a long-term commitment to our common endeavors, to fighting terrorism and building democratic states with viable political institutions that can redress that can address the aspirations of the people there.

So I'd like to see this assistance continue, but I'd like it to be committed to a democratic Pakistan. I find it very strange that democracies should be supported in Afghanistan, and yet while democratic leaders in Afghanistan give confidence to the international community, the international community is still apprehensive about dealing with democratic leaders in Pakistan.

For me, I see military rule as the problem. I don't see it as the solution.

HAASS: But just to be clear, so we understand what you're saying, are you therefore suggesting that Congress or others should reduce U.S. aid to Pakistan unless democracy is restored?

BHUTTO: Well, I would like them to link it to the restoration of democracy, yes. I think they need to tell our military has a vested interest in seeing a restoration of democracy. Most of the people in our army are patriotic. Most of the people in our army would not like to see any harm come to our country. And if they feel that the aid is going to dry up, they'll have an institutional interest in promoting democracy to keep the aid coming in. But if they think that they can keep the aid even with the dictatorship, why should they tilt towards a democracy?

HAASS: I want to call on Dan Markey, who's our senior fellow here for India, Pakistan and South Asia .

QUESTIONER: Hi. You mentioned one silver lining in all of these challenges, and that was the chief justice and his restoration, the protests that led up to that. And I'm curious how you understand that. Do you see it as a kind of one political moment, sort of a bump in the road, or is this a fundamental turning point for Pakistan? Is this something much more historic, something much more lasting? Does it have more potential?

BHUTTO: It's too early to say whether this will be a lasting phenomenon. But certainly for many Pakistanis it has given hope that it could turn into a defining moment when the judiciary finally begins to operate independently.

The chief justice's return, for example, has enabled my party to go to the court to seek relief where the electoral lists were concerned for the forthcoming elections. Thirty percent of our voters were not enrolled. Of those that were enrolled, 26 percent were duplicates. So we have a hope of having an independent adjudicator.

Mr. Nawaz Sharif has also filed a petition seeking to return to Pakistan. The lawyers movement is the lawyers community is highly energized. Many people lost their lives in the struggle. Many were imprisoned. A heavy price was paid. They were baton charged, had head injuries.

So, given this mood in the country, we hope that it can become a permanent turning point in our country's history. It's certainly given hope.

HAASS: One of the series we have here at the council is called Lessons Learned, where we ask prominent individuals to reflect on their careers and decisions they've made, all of which is a segue to this probably last question from Trudy Rubin, who's with the Philadelphia Inquirer. And she basically says: If you became prime minister again, what would you do differently? What are the lessons that you learned from your two stints in political power and now as an observer on the outside?

BHUTTO: Well, you know, in retrospect, you look back and you see things with a different vision, and there were certainly things I wish I had done differently. For example, I was with my father at Shimla when he signed the Shimla agreement with India to try and bring the two countries to peace despite the differences on Kashmir. And it was always my dream to be remembered as to give a legacy as a peacemaker. So I do look back in retrospect and regret the opportunity I had to make peace.

Secondly, I remember when the Taliban first came up in neighboring Afghanistan. Many of us, including our friends from the U.S., initially thought that they would bring peace to that war-torn country. And that was a critical, fatal mistake we made. If I had to do things again, that's certainly not a decision that I would have taken.

And in my early years, I think, as one of the first female, woman prime ministers in a Muslim world and one of the first group of women leaders on the world stage, I was so concerned with trying to appear as tough as a man and as strong as a man, and to judge myself to be a good leader by such decisions. I don't think I would have been as I think I should have been true to what I was. The people wanted me to be there as a woman leader, somebody who was more nurturing, who could take care of our people, our women, our children, redress their needs, build them hostels and schools and provide them with basic nutrition. I wish I had focused more on that than on the more militaristic notions. All that militarization did not in the end save us at Kargil. It took President Clinton to bring an end to that particular phase.

So, yes, you look back and you see many things that you would have done differently.

HAASS: Thank you. It seems a fitting place.

Let me just say this is, again, a rare meeting in August. They will resume with a rather busy schedule, and particularly in September when we have all sorts of leaders coming to New York for the U.N. General Assembly.

Let me again thank you all for coming and apologize to those for whose desire to ask questions did not get realized. Please don't hate me through Labor Day.

BHUTTO: Thank you, Richard. Thank you very much. Thank you. I hope it won't take you 30 years to invite me again.

HAASS: No chance.

6

PAKISTAN PEOPLE PARTY

History

Pakistan People's Party (PPP) was founded at Lahore at a convention held on 28th November, 1967. The charismatic Leader, Mr. Zulfiqar Ali Bhutto was unanimously elected as the Chairman of the party. A number of Foundation Documents was adopted enunciating the Party Creed which was summarized as follows:

- Islam is their Faith
- Democracy is their Politics
- Socialism is their Economy
- All Power to the People

This blend of Islam and Socialism steered a course away from Secular Dogmatic Marxism and came to be known as Islamic Socialism.

Until the formation of the Pakistan People's Party power in Pakistan may have changed hands but remained within the same elite. The socialist parties of different hue had not penetrated the masses, enjoyed scant electoral support and even less representation in the assemblies.

The PPP attracted the active participation of the peasants, workers and middle class.

At the time the Party was founded, Pakistan was under the yoke of the Ayub Khan regime and governed by the Constitution of Pakistan 1962. Under the Constitution power was concentrated in the President, elected members of the National and Provincial Assemblies were debarred from holding Ministerial offices and the elections to the office of the President and the Assemblies were conducted through 80,000 Basic Democrats who constituted an electoral college which could be, and was, manipulated to perpetuate the rule of the Convention Muslim League presided by Ayub Khan.

Neither the Basic Democracy nor the Presidential system was in accord with the political culture of Pakistan. There was a universal demand for a parliamentary system based on adult franchise which took the form of a movement in the winter of 1968-69, which overthrew Ayub Khan. Ayub Khan's successor, General Yahya Khan, held the first general elections based on adult franchise at the end of 1970. The Awami League, led by Sheikh Mujeeb ur Rehman, swept the polls in East Pakistan on a six-point agenda of autonomy which fell barely short of secession while the Pakistan People's Party emerged triumphant in the Western wing of the country on the basis of its socialist programme of vesting the commanding heights of the economy under state control. The slogan of "Food, Shelter and Clothing" for the masses-became the hall mark of the party.

A civil war broke out during 1971 in the aftermath of the election and the province of East Pakistan emerged as the new state of Bangladesh from that blood soaked trauma. In the wake of the fall of Dacca, Yahya Khan handed over power to Zulfiqar Ali Bhutto as President on 20th December 1971. Bhutto first moved fast to introduce a Provisional Constitution and to lift Martial Law in April, 1972 followed by a permanent Constitution of 1973, passed unanimously, the lasting legacy of the Pakistan People's Party to Pakistan.

Bhutto administration was an age of reform and reconstruction. Bhutto established Pakistan's first Steel Mill, a second Port, commissioned Pakistan's first hydro-electric dam on the mighty Indus at Tarbela, and made Pakistan self sufficient in fertilizer, sugar, and cement. He nationalized the banks and life insurance companies. He also initiated Pakistan's Nuclear Programme. The economical policies of Bhutto were anti-imperialist and based on state socialism following the mound of other Third World leaders such as Gamal Abdel Nasser of Egypt, Ahmad Soekarno of Indonesia, and his own contemporary Salvador Allende of Chile who was elected, overthrown and assassinated during the same period. The Cold War was its most frosty during this epoch. The Neo-Colonialists made a horrible example of Bhutto for his anti-Imperialistic stance, his efforts to unite the World of Islam, and his demarche towards bringing the Third World on one platform apart from the Nuclear Issue.

Disturbance following the elections of 1977, provided General Zia ul Haq, Chief of the Army Staff, an opportunity to overthrow the elected Prime Minister and later manipulated for his execution by a hung Court in which the real majority was in favour of acquittal, two of the acquitting Judges having been forced into retirement by Zia.

The whiplash of the Martial Law fell heavily on the Pakistan People's Party from July 5, 1977 when Zia declared Martial Law until December 1985, when Martial Law was lifted. Thousands of the cadre of the Pakistan People's Party were incarcerated, hundreds whipped, including ex-Minister and Members of the Assemblies. Others were killed or forced into exile.

The police lathicharged Begum Bhutto who had been elected the Acting Chairperson of the Party following the arrest of Zulfiqar Ali Bhutto in September, 1977 and cracked her skull leaving her bleeding to death. As a result of long periods of incarceration in unhygienic conditions Benazir Bhutto who was elected as Chairperson of the party, following the disqualification of Begum Nusrat Bhutto, in February, 1978, has been left permanently impaired in hearing.

Benazir Bhutto rescued and rebuilt the party from scratch, leading an epic movement for the restoration of democracy. Her historical welcome in Lahore in April, 1986 was the turn of the tide. In the meanwhile Zia was digging his own grave. He dismissed his handpicked protégé Muhammad Khan Jonejo and dissolved the National Assembly of Pakistan on May 29, 1988. Zia probably wanted to revert to the Ayub's regime. A few days before his death, while revealing his plans for a Presidential system, he told a confidante " I will be around a long time". Fate intervened on 17th August, 1988 when the C-130, carrying him crashed in a ball of fire and Zia went from ashes to ashes and his system from dust to dust.

Benazir Bhutto rode the crest of the wave to victory to become the youngest and first Muslim woman Prime Minister at the age of 35. During both her terms as Prime Minister, Benazir Bhutto was betrayed by Presidents elected with her party votes, first by Ghulam Ishaq Khan and later by her close party protégé Farooq Ahmad Khan Leghari, who dismissed her Governments in 1990 and 1993 respectively. She never enjoyed the uninterrupted five years spell in power, which is the right of Government in Pakistan.

By the time Benazir Bhutto was first elected, the Cold War was over, the General Accord had been signed; and the Soviet withdrawal from Afghanistan had begun. The times had changed further when she was elected for the second time in 1993—the Soviet Union itself had disintegrated and Germany united. The very country which had introduced the system of a state controlled economy as a shortcut to development, is in the depth of recession and floundering its way to a market economy.

Benazir Bhutto redefined the party programme at the silver jubilee of the party at Lahore in November, 1992. The

New Social Contract of Benazir Bhutto is predicated upon a social market economy, privatization of the means of production, down sizing of the Government, devolution of power to the Province; and decentralization to Local Government.

In the aftermath of the 1997 election, Pakistan has fallen into the grip of a civilian dictatorship and the Muslim League into the clutches of the Sharif family. With the help of the Sharifs, a protégé of Zia, the Constitution has been amended. Taking advantage of the nuclear tests of May 28, the Government has proclaimed an Emergency which enables the Federal Government to impose a unitary form of Government by arrogating the powers of the Provincial Governments to itself. The power has already been exercised by enforcing Federal Rule upon the Province of Sindh , the country's second largest Province, where the Muslim League is a minority Party with less than a fifth of the seats in the Provincial Assembly of Sindh. A similar threat looms large on the North West Frontier Province where the Muslim League minority Government has parted ways with the traditionally strong Awami National Party. The Government of the Baluchistan National Party led by Akhtar Mengal, has already been over thrown.

In a bid to concentrate powers in their family, the Sharif brothers have maneuvered the passage of the Shariat Bill i.e. the 15th Amendment (CA 15) in the National Assembly which is stalled in the Senate by the PPP and most of the regional parties.

The PPP has forged links with the anti-fascist forces which are attempting to impose a unitary Government in Pakistan with the aid of an Emergency which provides a lame excuse for usurpation of the rights of Provinces. The CA 15 would empower the Sharif's to rule by Decree by-passing parliament and the courts. In this new scenario the PPP has emerged as a party advocating a Federal Liberal Democracy and a social market economy: On the lines of Social Democratic Parties of Europe. This is reflected in the 10 Point Programme announced by Benazir Bhutto in the Autumn of 1998.

Manifesto Aim

It is a birthright too often snatched at the point of the gun from the citizens by the very men who are to guard and defend us. This can stop to enable the people and the country to march with confidence and courage, with pride and dignity, with progress and prosperity into the twenty first century.

Pakistan is a great Federation. Its multilingual, multicultural society is its strength. Its sons and daughters are its true assets, the bright face of its future, the promise of all their tomorrows.

The Pakistan Peoples Party is the only Federal, democratic and equal opportunity Party that can guarantee to their great people a great future. The PPP worker is selfless and committed to the values of Faith, freedom, fundamental human rights, family values and a wholesome society based on the rule of law and human dignity.

The founding principle of the Party Islam is their religion places a responsibility on each PPP supporter to reach out in a spirit of accommodation and tolerance to all faiths, to prevent the state from interfering in the religious rights of the citizens (which breeds sectarianism) and to treat people of all faiths with respect enabling them to enjoy religious freedom and equality before the law.

The second principle of the PPP ideology is that democracy is their policy. The PPP commitment to freedom and fundamental rights, including freedom from hunger and want, is written in the blood of its martyrs and in the red marks of lashes on the back of its workers. It is written in the suffering and sacrifice of its leaders the greatest of whom was Quaid e Awam. He faced the gallows refusing to bow before tyranny defending the human rights of their citizens to the last of his breath.

7

Her Manifesto for 2008 Elections

This Manifesto is our sacred pledge to the people of Pakistan, and most importantly to the children of Pakistan who are our future.

Pakistan faces a choice between Quaid-e-Azam's vision of a vibrant, tolerant and strong federation, and obscurantism and fragmentation

Pakistan faces a choice between Quaid-e-Awam's dream of a just society, and growing inequalities Pakistan faces a choice between hope and despair

Pakistan faces a choice between strength and uncertainty

Pakistan faces a choice between moving forward and looking back Pakistan faces a choice between progress for all and prosperity for a few

They choose Quaid-e-Azam's vision of tolerance, vibrance and harmony among provinces we choose Quaid-e-Awam's dream of a just society

They chose hope we chose strength they choose moving forward They choose progress for all

Basic Principles of the Party

The first principle of the Party is: **Islam is our Faith**. Islam teaches brotherhood, love and peace. Their faith places a responsibility on each citizen to reach out in a spirit of accommodation and tolerance to all religions and sects and to treat people of all faiths with respect, enabling them to enjoy religious freedom and equality before the law.

The message of Islam is the message of peace. It is a message of brotherhood and tolerance. These are symbolised in the words and verses of Data Sahib, Shah Abdul Latif of Bhittai, Baba Farid Ganj Shakar and Lal Shahbaz Qalander.

The sufi saints adopted a life of simple living and high thinking. It's time we did the same. By no means did they use or preach the use of force. The PPP commits itself to religious tolerance. Religious beliefs of individual citizens have little to do with the business of the state, as the Founder of the Nation declared in his inaugural address to the Constituent Assembly on 11 August 1947. The second principle of the PPP is: **Democracy is our Politics**. The PPP's commitment to freedom and fundamental rights, including freedom from hunger and want, is written in the blood of its martyrs and in the red marks of lashes on the back of its workers. It is written in the suffering and sacrifice of Quaid-e-Awam, who faced the gallows refusing to bow before tyranny, defending the human rights of our citizens to the last breath. In every age, including today, the PPP leaders and office bearers have been behind bars, in exile, facing political persecution, defending their Party at great personal cost to their families and themselves.

The third PPP principle is: **Social Democracy is our Economy**. The PPP aims at creating a just and equitable society with equal opportunity for all its citizens. The growing gap between the rich and the poor must be bridged by supporting the underprivileged, the downtrodden and the discriminated. The PPP is proud of being the voice of the poor, the working classes and the middle classes. Their policies, while dedicated to the underprivileged, created conditions that enabled the business and trading classes to compete in the open market. The party will foster a social market economy, a partnership of the public and private sectors, predicated upon a synthesis of economic liberalism with a strong social democratic agenda of State responsibilities for satisfying basic human needs: full employment, national health, universal education, water supply and sanitation.

The PPP reiterates its firm commitment to provide food, clothing and shelter *(Roti, Kapra Aur Makaan)* to every poor family in Pakistan through our unique emphasis on full employment. The PPP is the only party with a coherent vision of a welfare state for Pakistan where market forces are balanced with safety nets for the underprivileged and the poor.

The final principle of the PPP is **All Power to the People**. Only the people have the right on earth to determine their destiny and chart the course of their nation. All organs of State must be answerable to the Court of the people in an election or through their legitimately elected representatives in Parliament.

To the people of Pakistan we make the following Promises:

1. They Promise to rid Pakistan of violence, bigotry and terror,
2. They Promise the youth of Pakistan gainful employment, hope and opportunity,
3. They Promise to lower inflation,
4. They Promise to provide quality education and health care, and clean drinking water, to the masses,
5. They Promise to bring progress to the doorstep of the workers, farmers and small businesses,
6. They Promise to protect and support the disadvantaged and the vulnerable,
7. They Promise to make Pakistan a business friendly country,
8. They Promise to give high priority to empowerment of women and ensure their equal rights,
9. They Promise to put Pakistan on a sustainable high growth path,
10. They Promise to ensure sound macro-economic policies,

11. They Promise to ensure a strong Defence,
12. They Promise to ensure that energy shortages are eliminated,
13. They Promise to protect the Environment,
14. They Promise to ensure a world class irrigation system and sound use of scarce water,
15. They Promise to enhance Provincial Autonomy,
16. They Promise to put in place a citizen-centric government, and
17. Finally, They Promise Good Governance.

State of the Nation

Under the PPP Government, the country was hailed as an emerging capital market of the world. Since the dismissal of the PPP Government in 1996, Pakistan has been associated with terrorism, militancy and extremism. The crisis that began with the dismissal of the PPP government can only end with the return of the PPP, and through the masses, to government.

During the first decade of the 21st century, the country has suffered:

1. Dangerous increase in terrorism and suicide bombings,
2. Very high levels of poverty, unemployment, and inflation,
3. Failed poverty reduction program, and severe exclusion of poor from the benefits of growth and progress,
4. Undermined national integration with the increased level of discord among Provinces,
5. Abuse of institutions and the judiciary,
6. Obscurantism and hate among religious and ethnic groups,
7. Huge power shortages and increasing water scarcity, and
8. Increasing crime and suicides.

The present regime has eroded all national institutions. Its repression and oppression have created a culture of lawlessness and tyranny, inflicting misery in the lives of the people of Pakistan. There is no justice for the weak and the poor. The youth are unemployed, the farmers neglected, labour retrenched, stock markets manipulated, public sector units plundered, national resources squandered, the media muzzled, civil society attacked, judiciary crushed, and political leaders exiled, imprisoned and maligned.

Different areas of the country have been parcelled out to violent militant groups whose influence is spreading like a cancer throughout society. To stop the slide into lawlessness, extremism, anarchy, chaos, poverty and hunger, the restoration of genuine democracy, through free and fair elections is essential. The PPP symbolises the empowerment of the people of Pakistan. The PPP governments served the people. The world praised its energy programme as a model for the developing countries. The World Health Organisation gave the PPP government a Gold Medal in recognition of its contribution to the health of its people. The International Labour Organisation noted that the largest job-generation in the history of Pakistan took place under the PPP

As the voice of the people, the PPP is viewed with hostility by the anti-people forces who have rigged elections and destabilized governments to seize power and exploit the People and the Provinces of the country.

The social and living standards of the people are pathetic. While poverty decreased under the PPP government, poverty has increased over the years, as reported by the Economic Survey of Pakistan 2007.

Quaid-e-Awam made education compulsory for children, and built schools, colleges and universities. He took the literacy rate up to 26 per cent where it stagnated for a decade. Then Mohtarma Benazir Bhutto was elected and the literacy rate doubled to over 50 per cent. After the dismissal of the PPP government in 1996, education once again stagnated.

What is to be done?

The PPP promises change through

1. Employment
2. Education
3. Energy
4. Environment
5. Equality

The PPP believes in every individual's right to food, clothing, housing and an adequate livelihood. Their commitment to the people of Pakistan is that their basic rights are our responsibility. The party has, and will always, strive for the rights of the people.

The PPP slogan is Ilm, Roshni Sab Ko Kaam, Roti Kapra Aur Makaan, Maang Raha Hai Har Insaan.

It is not just an election between the PPP and other parties. It is a clash of sharply competing values and ideologies. The PPP is a party truly born out of the hearts and minds of the workers, peasants, small business, and the vast majority of citizens who support the Islamic spirit of tolerance and social justice, and not a party that is born out of backroom deals in agency offices.

- They are the Party that derives its strength from each and every section of a pluralistic society. They are the Party whose philosophy is rooted in combining sustainable economic growth with social justice.
- They are the Party that recognizes that this is a moment to consolidate all the forces that subscribe to the true spirit of Islam, and fundamental values of federalism and democracy.
- The PPP's mission is to transform the lives of our people from one of despair and poverty into one of hope and opportunity through employment, education, energy, environment and equality.
- They have a clear and coherent vision of what needs to be done and will muster all the resources to get it done.

- They will take a new approach marked by a determination to challenge the threats and not ignore them.
- They renew our commitment to build a hopeful future for the poverty stricken.
- They will strive for a Pakistan where all, rather than some, live in comfort and plenty.
- They will strive for a Pakistan where everyone is included in the expanding circle of development. They will, with vigour and determination, assure basic needs for all citizens.
- They will strive to have a responsive, responsible and representative government at all levels. Social and economic justice is the defining objective of the PPP's policy framework. They will reduce social and economic inequalities between various classes, between Provinces, within Provinces, and genders, establishing a just society. National policy frameworks have, to date, accorded primacy to economic policy goals, with social policy goals not pursued aggressively. Even within economic policy-making, employment has not been a major objective. Resultantly, social and human development indicators have continued to lag behind woefully. The very objective of development has remained unfulfilled.

The Pakistan People's Party proposes to reverse the order of priorities; whereby social policy objectives drive economic policy. Development shall be measured in terms of the welfare of the people, rather than in terms of financial statistics that do not reflect the state of the nation. Employment and social and human development shall be specific targets in policymaking and economic policy measures will be geared to achieve social goals.

The twin menace of inflation and unemployment are to be specifically tackled.

The PPP will help individuals set up small businesses and provide the framework for a vibrant middle class. It will address the basic needs of low-income persons.

Growth with Equity

PPP governments since 1967 gave birth to boom economies. In its last tenure, the PPP tripled economic growth rates, doubled taxation receipts and took agricultural growth rates from zero to seven percent annually. It reduced the budget deficit and paid off principal debt while investing in a massive socio-economic program. The PPP, as a modern and moderate party, attracted four times more direct private sector investment in three years than all of Pakistan's previous governments, creating jobs and wealth for the people of Pakistan.

The PPP computerized the State Bank of Pakistan and the Stock Market, introduced the National Identity Cards scheme and deregulated, decentralized and privatised the economy.

The PPP power projects and mass telephone system enabled ordinary people to set up businesses when previously power shutdowns and twenty year delays for telephones prevented them from success in private initiatives.

Open Minds, Open Markets, Open Opportunities is our slogan as we change IOUs into MOUs. They believe that markets, not missiles, are the measure of might.

The PPP government will accelerate growth, for only with high growth can the social policy objectives of poverty reduction and high employment be achieved.

The key pillars of the equitable and pro-poor growth agenda comprise: Rapid Economic Growth; Combating Unemployment; Targeted Poverty Programmes; Just Labour Policies; Private Sector as Engine of Growth; Accelerating Agricultural and Rural Growth, and Ensuring Water Security and Energy Infrastructure.

Rapid Economic Growth

PPP will be a fiscally responsible government, ensuring that taxpayers get their full value for the taxes they pay.

A Sound Debt Policy

They will ensure that we do not burden future generations with excessive debt. With that in mind, we will ensure that domestic and external debt is maintained at sustainable levels.

PPP was the first government in the history of Pakistan to retire Pakistan's principal debt through the proceeds of privatisation. The PPP will stop raising domestic and foreign debt for wasteful projects and use the fiscal space provided by the rescheduling of loans and the international assistance for fighting the war against terrorism for the national benefit. Where needed, the PPP will aggressively seek to use the fiscal space to retire expensive domestic and foreign debt. The aim of the PPP is to make Pakistan into a self respecting, self reliant nation whose citizens are honoured universally.

Containing Inflation

High inflation is a major economic problem of Pakistan, especially hurting the low income groups. At the macro level, containing inflation will be achieved through prudent monetary and fiscal policies. In addition, the following specific measures will be considered:

1. Special steps to increase production of foodgrains, including creating an enabling environment so that greater private sector credit flows towards these sectors.
2. Enhancing competition, in both manufacturing and domestic trade, and reducing supply chain constraints so that costs of essential goods are reduced. To this end, the Securities and Exchange Commission of Pakistan (SECP) will be strengthened to unleash competitive forces, and aggressively combat monopolies and cartels
3. Create effective institutions at Federal, Provincial and District levels to monitor supply positions of essential commodities to ensure prompt remedial measures.

4. Maintain strategic stocks of wheat and other essential commodities to overcome shortages, while ensuring that fiscal costs are manageable and waste/corruption is eliminated.

Establishing a Fair Tax System

The Party is determined to overhaul the taxation system and bring about changes which will lead to fair practices, rational tax slab, curtailment of discretionary powers and growth of business and industry. The tax system will be made tax payer friendly so that voluntary compliance is enhanced. The PPP commits itself to rationalizing the taxation system so that the burden of tax on the poor and low income groups is reduced, while at the same time Tax/GDP ratio is increased. PPP recognizes that Tax/GDP needs to be increased to provide adequate resources for providing good quality services to all people and for Pakistan to have the necessary infrastructure to sustain high growth. To that end, bold initiatives will be taken emphasising better collection and expanding the tax net, especially to those that can afford to pay.

Combating Unemployment

The PPP will put in place bold and innovative programmes to create jobs in the public and private sector. PPP fully recognizes that high growth will be the main driver of full employment. At the same time, the PPP will establish programmes to help those who are unable to find gainful employment. A four-pronged strategy will be used to provide income earning opportunities to the poor as well as unemployed youth. The strategy comprises:

Public Works Programme (PWP)

A labour-intensive PWP will be put in place so that there is guaranteed employment, of at least one year, to one working member of the poorest 25 per cent families of Pakistan.

The PWP will expand labour-intensive civil works in infrastructure, sanitation, road works, water and irrigation; with a view to providing large-scale employment in rural and urban areas. These schemes will be communitydriven and managed.

Literacy and Health Corps (LHC) Unemployment amongst educated youth has assumed alarming proportions. With twin objectives of providing short-term employment to educated youth, and to assist with social policy goals, a Literacy and Health Corps Scheme will be established. Under the scheme, there will be an employment guarantee of two years to all youth completing intermediate, graduation and post graduation in a given year. A large proportion of the jobs will be in the social sectors (elementary education and basic health-care) and will form part of the PPP's programme for the expansion of social services. This will constitute a basic literacy and health corps in the service of the nation.

Vocational Training

The PPP will put in place programs, which offer the youth Vocational Education and Technical Training in those service sectors where there is a shortage in the market.

Microfinance

The PPP government under Mohtarma Benazir Bhutto introduced microfinance institutions in Pakistan to provide self employment. This programme will be doubled. Appropriate microfinance policy and institutional reforms will be put in place so that commercial banks, micro-finance institutions and NGOs aggressively increase their outreach to meet the goal of 5 million beneficiaries on a sustainable basis.

Targeted Poverty Programmes

The PPP is committed to assist those that are bypassed by growth and development, especially the vulnerable and disadvantaged. It will put in place a comprehensive Targeted Anti-Poverty Programe, comprising the following strands:

1. Conditional Cash Transfers, which transfer cash subsidies to poor families in return for sending children (especially girls) to school and getting children inoculated.
2. Strengthening and expansion of social protection programs, such as Zakat, Social Security, Baitul Mal, worker-retraining and mobility
3. Special Programme for the least developed (lowest 50%) Districts to improve access to social services
4. The PPP will look after the senior citizens of our land; amongst other measures, we will provide financial support to all senior citizens above the age of 65 years who have no source of income.
5. The PPP will establish a database of the poorest 25 per cent of families, so that these programmes can be properly targeted.

Just Labour Policies

For high levels of Employment, equitable growth is crucial and Pakistan needs to have a labour policy that is in line with the ILO standards.

To protect the basic rights of workers, the PPP will initiate the following policies:

1. The Industrial Relations Ordinance 2002 will be reviewed to bring it in conformity with the ILO Conventions, ratified by Pakistan, and Fundamental Rights guaranteed by the Constitution of Pakistan.
2. The EOBI and other labour welfare programs will be strengthened and public-private partnerships established, so that labour and their families have access to quality education, health care and affordable housing.
3. Review of the President's Special Powers of Removal from Service Ordinance 2000 with regards to trade union activities.
4. Elimination of child labour, forced labour and bonded labour, and education and rehabilitation of those children once withdrawn from the workplaces.

5. Enforcement of statutory labour laws, through effective inspection systems.
6. Regularly holding National Tripartite Labour Conference to formulate labour, economic and social policies and to devise mechanisms for their effective implementation with a view to promoting social justice, decent work and raising the dignity of labour.
7. Developing a safety culture for making work safe and prevention of accidents at workplaces and occupational diseases of workers.
8. Minimum wage will be enhanced to meet the escalating needs of labour.

Private Sector as Engine of Growth, the PPP is committed to ensuring that Private Sector and export-led development will be the main engine of growth. The government will embark on an aggressive Investment Climate Reforms Programme to establish a favourable and enabling environment so that all businesses, foreign and domestic, flourish. The Party will improve the investment climate especially for Small and MicroBusinesses, initiate programs to reduce cost of doing business and increase Pakistan's competitiveness, streamline government business interface through aggressive deregulation, and seek Foreign Direct Investment (FDI) in export manufacturing.

The Pakistan People's Party will confine the role of the public sector in health, education and infrastructure. The role of the State will be restricted only to those areas where the private sector is not forthcoming.

A special programme will be developed to attract the financial resources and special skills of Pakistani Diaspora and overseas workers, with a view to contribute to the national development efforts. Privatisation was introduced by the first government of Prime Minister Benazir Bhutto, elected in 1988. This will be continued in a transparent manner, ensuring that labour is a beneficiary of the process. The PPP will vigorously pursue a policy of diversification of industrial exports and manufactured products. The emphasis will be on adding value to primary products and raw materials. The PPP Government will provide market-based and fiscally affordable incentives to develop non-traditional exports.

They will also provide incentives to raise the level of technology in our industries.

An important pillar of our private sector development will be an aggressive program to foster and encourage Small and Medium Enterpries (SMEs), recognizing that these provide the bulk of employment. Programmes and policies will be put in place to reduce the regulatory burden on SMEs and enhance the voluntary flow of credit to these businesses.

Accelerating Agriculture and Rural Growth Agriculture is the mainstay of the National Economy of Pakistan. As a farmer-friendly party, the PPP will help farmers boost production and obtain fair prices. Farmers got the best prices when the PPP was in government. The key to agricultural exportable surpluses is to augment the output per acre and productivity per farmer.

Aggressive Agriculture and Rural Development will be another central pillar of our growth and poverty reduction strategy. Their efforts will be focused on improving productivity and crop diversification, agricultural markets and exports, and special programs for small farmers to reduce risks faced by them. Moreover, with advances in technology the desert can be made green.

The Pakistani peasant, mired in poverty and debt has to be rescued from the morass of despair by a bold policy which ensures that the private sector provides key inputs and services -such as credit, fertilizer, pesticides, extension, marketing, seeds, tractors-in a timely manner and at competitive prices.

Special attention would be given to encouraging Banks to expand rural lending, while maintaining sound credit policies.

Special capacity-building programs for agricultural support services will be put in place to revitalize key institutions of research and extension.

A sustainable programme of farm to market roads will be put in place to ensure that perishable and valuable agricultural products like fruits; vegetables and milk can reach markets to enable better incomes for farmers and for the benefit of urban consumers. Pakistan People's Party commits itself to providing all surplus electric power during off peak hours for tube-wells free of cost

Ensuring Water Security

The PPP government is committed to ensuring water security for irrigation and availability of clean drinking water.

Pakistan is now a water scarce country. Scarcity will increase with time, with a burgeoning population and climate change. The PPP will put in place a bold and comprehensive program to ensure water security for future generations. Key elements of the strategy would consist of: water conservation, additional storages, farmer-managed irrigation systems, rehabilitation of the ageing canal and barrage system, an effective drainage system, enhancing water productivity, strengthening water rights and protecting the lower delta eco-systems. In respect of the Arid Zones, a program will be developed to harness water from rain and flash floods, promote drip irrigation and crops that need less water.

Clean drinking water is a basic need. The PPP shall create a legal framework to ensure availability of clean drinking water for all.

Ensuring Energy Infrastructure

The consumption of electricity is an index of economic prosperity. Pakistan's per capita electricity consumption is about one-tenth of the world average. The last power station established in the public sector was the PPP's Ghazi Barotha 1450MW hydro electric power project which went online in 2004. The PPP also obtained a 500 MW nuclear power station at Chasma. The PPP government inducted over 5000MW of private power generation, ending shutdowns. Now Pakistan needs another 8000 MWs by 2010 to meet the energy requirements of the people. This will be met by utilising coal, solar, hydro and wind power.

The PPP is committed to establishing a comprehensive and credible programme that ensures energy security and adequacy of supply. Key elements would include: maximum use of indigenous water and hydrocarbon resources, energy conservation, proper pricing to ensure proper use while protecting the life line consumers. Specific actions and interventions will include encouraging and attracting private sector energy projects, fast tracking of exploration and development of indigenous hydro-carbon resources, including the Thar coal project, accelerating development of alternative energy, including wind and solar energy, reviving the Keti Bunder project, establishing an energy corridor from Central Asia to Balochistan, and a sustainable program to bring energy to the doorstep of the poor.

Fisheries

The PPP will establish programmes that will provide training and micro-credit facilities to the fisher folks and ensure proper facilities, infrastructure to increase export potential of this sector in keeping with international standards.

Growth-Inducing Transport Infrastructure Development

The PPP will develop and implement a national transport development program, to sustain high growth, improve access to rural areas and to reduce internal logistics costs and downtime, especially for exports. In particular, it would establish a world class North South Transport corridor.

Meeting Basic Needs of Pakistan People

Empowerment and social change will be another cornerstone of the PPP's Agenda for change. Using the full resources of the Government, private sector and community organizations, a social transformation programme will be ushered.

Education

The Pakistan People's Party built 48,000 schools in its two tenures between 1988 to 1996; it recruited and trained 100,000 teachers in three years alone, thereby doubling literacy.

The PPP increased the education budget by many billions in its last two recent tenures of power, a testimony to the top priority it gives to education. The PPP commits to its sons and daughters of Pakistan an education system that enables a brighter future than that of their parents so that they can hold their heads high in the comity of Nations.

Quaid-e-Awam introduced free and compulsory primary education, promoted Centres of Excellence, created Institutes of Science and Technology and took Pakistan to the cutting edge of Nuclear Physics, establishing centres of Nuclear Medicine. He set up a chain of new Universities, Medical and Engineering Colleges in the neglected areas as a harbinger to a Muslim Renaissance.

The PPP will focus on providing computers progressively for every secondary school and college in Pakistan. The Party will install at least one computer in each school so that the new generation can enter the digital age.

To universalize basic education, every child in government primary schools will be provided a stipend.

Universal enrolment by 2015 of all children between the ages of 5 to 10 is the target of the Party.

The Pakistan People's Party believes in providing quality higher education in all regions of Pakistan through both public and private sector colleges, universities and Institutes. The quality of existing colleges and universities will be improved and the number of public universities and colleges, particularly in Science and Engineering, Medicine and Agriculture will be increased. Funding will be regulated and monitored through Quality Assurance Boards of the Higher Education Commission. Funding to Private Sector Universities will be enhanced through a competitive programme.

Madrassa Reforms

They are in the process of sowing the seeds of national disintegration of a new generation of alienated young people bred on hate and paranoia. Educational extremism thus represents the greatest danger to Quaid-e-Azam's vision of the federation.

The funding of groups during Afghan Jihad of the '80s has led to the rise of political madrassas. Many of them are not schools but irregular army recruitment centres for militants as well as arm depots holding rocket launchers and Kalashnikov guns. No militia will be allowed to seek refuge under the name of madrassahs for militant activities. Madrassas will be reformed to be Madrassas that impart knowledge to children. The PPP had planned to build *'Apna Ghar'* (Their Home) as a free boarding school for socially or economically disadvantaged children. The plan initially adopted by the PPP in the budget of 1996, but dropped by subsequent governments, will be revived.

Student Militancy

The PPP will lift the ban on student unions as it has done in all its tenures. It will not permit arms on campus.

Health of the Nation

All PPP Governments have made health a high priority, believing that the welfare of people flows from investing in the health of the people. Basic Principles of the Health Policy are: First, the Guarantee of Access to a Doctor for every Citizen of Pakistan via a National Health Service; Second, the Prevention of Disease; Third, the Guarantee that Affordable Medicines are available to the sick and needy; Fourth, the provision of good Medical Education and Training.

The Lady Health Workers (LHW) programme initiated by the PPP government has been the most successful initiative in the preventive health sector in the last two decades; it increased contraceptive prevalence and reduced mother and child mortality ratios. The PPP will further consolidate this programme and take the number of LHWs up to 200,000 in the next 5 years, extending it to *Katchi Abadis* in urban areas. A scheme for inducting 10,000 male health workers will be introduced in parts of NWFP and Balochistan.

The party will initiate a media campaign on various aspects of preventive health measures to increase awareness on health, safe motherhood, hygiene and nutrition.

Access to quality drugs has eluded the poor citizens of this country. The Pakistan Peoples Party will initiate a pro-people Drugs policy for the Public Sector Health System and maintain prices within the reach of the common man for the WHO- approved list of 300 essential drugs. The PPP will introduce competitive measures to ensure parity with regional price levels.

As in other Muslim Countries, including Iran, Bangladesh and Indonesia, Pakistan aims to protect the health and care of both Mother and Child through Planned Parenthood.

Census

The PPP will hold a census every ten years and ensure that the Census results are accurate, enabling resource distribution equitably in the country.

Human Settlements

Historically, town planning is a concept developed by the ancient Indus Valley Civilization. To keep up with its glorious legacy, the PPP will invest in providing clean drinking water, sanitation and planning.

The Pakistan People's Party will set up a Human Settlements Commission to prepare a Master Plan of Human Settlements for the Whole Country including the needs for housing, roads, parks and playgrounds.

The Pakistan Peoples Party will assist Provincial and District Governments with establishing liveable cities and human settlements. The urban degradation that is taking place will be reversed with the provision of resources and capacity support.

Housing Policy

A house for every family is a key part of the PPP slogan *Maang Raha Hai Har Insaan, Roti Kapra Aur Makaan.*

A comprehensive and credible program will be developed and implemented to enable low and middle income families to own their own homes. Such a programme will comprise releasing government urban land, changes in zoning and land titling, changes in foreclosure laws, provision of long-term credit which is sustainable, and establishment of needed institutions, in the private and public sectors, to make the dream of home-ownership a reality for the masses.

Empowerment of Women

The Pakistan People's Party has an unflinching commitment to the cause of gender equality ever since it was founded in 1967. It is also the only Party in Pakistan that is headed by a woman. Mohtarma Benazir Bhutto was the first elected woman head of Government in the Muslim world.

1. The Party shall enunciate a national employment policy for Women, facilitating job creation and Women's participation in the economy. The 10% affirmative action job quota for Women in public service initiated by Mohtarma Benazir Bhutto's government will be increased to 20%.
2. Effective legislation to enable legal ownership of assets and resources for Women will be enacted to facilitate their financial independence.
3. The Party will take institutional initiatives to prevent crimes against Women in the name of tribalism, such as honour-killings and forced marriages.
4. Family Courts will be presided by Women Judges to hear Family Law Cases. Right of Maintenance and child custody according to law will be implemented.

5. Women will be appointed to the superior judiciary.
6. Ministry of Women Development will be part of important policy-making bodies to ensure that gender priorities are reflected in all policy initiatives.

Human Rights

As the Party that introduced a Ministry for Human Rights, the PPP will respect the life, liberty, property, livelihood and right to freedom of association, expression and movement of every citizen. It will honour the International Human Rights Declaration in both letter and spirit. The PPP will protect the rights in particular of the weak and oppressed, the discriminated and the downtrodden.

Minorities

To uplift and empower minorities, a job quota for minorities in the services of Pakistan, including the operational services like Army, Police, Intelligence Agencies, Judiciary and Foreign Affairs will be allocated.

An independent permanent National Commission for Religious Minorities will be instituted, with the powers of Tribunals which can entertain complaints and provide redress on urgent basis. Minorities will be given administrative control of their places of worship and a person belonging to a minority group will be made head of the Evacuee Trust Property Board.

The statutes that discriminate against religious Minorities, and are sources of communal disharmony, will be reviewed.

Information and Media

The Pakistan People's Party recognizes that a free and vibrant press is the greatest guarantor against tyranny and oppression. In accordance with this principle, the PPP liberated the press in 1988 by allowing free import of newsprint, the abolition of government permission to establish newspapers and journals, and by introducing

Private Radio and Television Stations. Each ministry will set up its own media cell to put across the point of view of the Ministry. Journalists from the private sector will be eligible for induction on contract basis and on competitive market rates.

A Press Complaints Commission will be established on the basis of the British system of Press Complaints. The Private Sector will be allowed to freely establish television and radio stations subject to their operating within a legal framework. FM stations licenses will be given to the Political Parties.

Information and Communication Technologies

The PPP heralded the information age into Pakistan with colour television, fax machines, emails and satellite television. It laid fibre optic lines in 1989 and digitalised telecommunications. In 1993, it began computer literacy programs to herald the computer literate generation. Software technology parks were to be established in the major cities by the PPP

The PPP fully supports the United Nations Information and Communication Technology Task Force (UNICTF) goals. Working with the UN, the PPP will create an enabling environment to map UN's Millennium Development Goals (MDGs). They believe that ICTs play an important role in development, poverty reduction, empowering women, reducing gender gap and communicating and practicing democratic values. They will replicate the best practices in Pakistan and will develop a comprehensive e-Government Strategy.

The PPP will implement an ICT policy and program to bridge the digital divide and to enable Pakistan to join the ranks of world leaders in IT. A comprehensive program will include: expanding telecommunications bandwidth capacity, expand training institutions for IT professionals, promotion of IT and software exports.

Science and Technology

The PPP gave the best science and technology institutions to the country. Science and Technology Hubs will be established in major urban areas, much like the science cities in the developed world.

Culture

The Pakistan People's Party will promote national heritage and culture of Pakistan. They will increase funding for the Arts, and support artists and their institutions.

Environment

They have inherited the earth to nourish and treasure, not to plunder and destroy.

The PPP will follow environment-friendly policies to build a cleaner, healthier environment for our children. Curriculum on environment will be introduced in schools.

- The PPP supports the Kyoto protocol on climate change.
- The PPP will accelerate programmes which will ensure Clean Air, Land, and Water for All.
- The PPP will introduce CNG units in major cities to reduce vehicular pollution.
- The PPP will set up a new National Calamities and Disaster Management Authority and make the Pakistan Environmental Protection Agency (PEPA) an autonomous authority.

Good Governance

Magna Carta of Pakistan, The Pakistan People's Party reaffirms its commitments to implement the Charter of Democracy; the veritable Magna Carta of Pakistan. As early as 1949, the Public Representatives Officers Disqualification Act (PRODA) was used for the ulterior purpose of driving out the Stalwarts of Muslim Leaders from the arena of Politics. The scythe of the Electoral Bodies Disqualification Order of 1960 decapitated the entire Founding Fathers of Pakistan.

Zia-ul Haq promulgated the Martial Law Order 17 of 1977 in order to victimize and disqualify the leadership of the Pakistan People's Party. In the most heinous deed of our tormented political history, Zia-ul Haq physically murdered his benefactor on April 4, 1979.

The so-called accountability measures since 1996 were used to incarcerate Senator Asif Ali Zardari for eight long years, although he and Mohtarma Benazir Bhutto were never sentenced for any crime. False cases were used in a conspiracy in an attempt to break their will to fight for the people of Pakistan and also to deceive the people of Pakistan about their legitimate democratic leadership.

The Supreme Court of Pakistan rightly observed in 1958: "When politics enters the Palace of Justice, Democracy, its cherished inmate, walks out of the backdoor. A Judge's duty in a given case is to adjudicate on the right or liability and this function he must discharge according to law. The Constitution entrusts the interests of the Country, in the appointment of a Prime Minister, to the members of the Parliament and if the country is ruined by the wrong choice of a Prime Minister, the responsibility is that of the people and their representatives and not of the Judge. The Judge's duty is to administer the law and not to lay down the moral or political standards for the choice of a Prime Minister."

The Charter consists of the following 36 points in brief:

1. The 1973 Constitution as on 12 October 1999 shall be restored save for the provisions of joint Electorates, reserved seats for Minorities and Women, lowering of the voting age to 18, and increase in seats in Parliament.
2. The appointment of Governors, three service Chiefs and the CJ SC shall be made by the Prime Minister who will be the Chief Executive.
3. The appointments of Judges to Superior Judiciary will be made with the advice and consent of a Joint Parliamentary Committee consisting of equal representatives of the Treasury and the Opposition on the recommendation of a Commission headed by

former Chief Justice who has not taken oath under the PCO.

4. A Federal Constitutional Court with equal representation to each Federating Unit will resolve Constitutional issues.
5. The Concurrent list will be abolished.
6. Reserved seats for Women will be allocated in proportion to percentage of votes polled by each contesting Party.
7. The strength of the Senate will be increased. 8. FATA will be merged into NWFP in consultation with the Tribal Areas.
9. Northern Areas will be given a Special Status and Empowerment.
10. Local Body elections will be held on Party Basis.
11. National Security Council will be abolished and replaced by Defence Committee headed by the Prime Minister.
12. The "ban" on Third term for Prime Minister will be scrapped.
13. Truth and Reconciliation Commission will be established.
14. Politically motivated NAB will be abolished and replaced by an Independent Accountability Commission whose Chairman will be appointed jointly by the Prime Minister and the Leader of the Opposition with the advice and consent of Joint Parliamentary Committee with parity between Treasury and the Opposition parties.
15. The Media will have freedom of access to Information regulated by Law.
16. The Chairman of the Public Accounts Committee will be appointed by the respective Leaders of the Opposition in the House.
17. Nuclear Command and Control will be placed under the Defence Committee of the Cabinet. 18. The future of Kashmir will be determined according to

the aspirations of the people of Kashmir and UN Resolutions.

19. Good Governance will include quality Health, Universal Education, Price Stability Employment Generation and Austerity by Government Officials.
20. Women, Minorities and under-privileged will be provided equality of opportunity.
21. Electorate mandate will be respected and extra constitutional ways will not be adopted for undermining the rights of the Government or Opposition.
22. Signatories to the Charter will not join Military regimes or sponsored Governments.
23. All indirect elections will be by open ballots. 24. All Military and Judicial Officers will file annual statements of Wealth and Income. 25. National Democracy Commission will promote Democratic Culture.
26. Terrorism and militancy will be vigorously confronted.
27. Impartiality and independence of the Election Commission will be guaranteed.
28. Elections will be held on a level-playing field. 29. Local Body Elections will be held within three months of General Elections.
30. Neutral administrators will be appointed by the Competent Election Authorities during the Conduct of elections.
31. Elections will be conducted by a neutral Caretaker Government.
32. All Security Agencies including ISI and MI will be answerable to the elected Prime Minister.
33. All indemnities promulgated by military regimes will be reviewed.
34. Defence Budget will be placed before and approved by Parliament.
35. Military Land and Cantonments will be controlled by the Ministry of Defence.

36. Rules of Business will be reviewed to conform to Parliamentary Traditions.

Provincial Autonomy

The Pakistan People's Party proposes to establish a true Federal Democracy in theory and practice by enacting the following reforms in order to make Provincial Autonomy meaningful.

The unanimous Constitution of 1973, authored by Quaid-e-Awam, introduced Provincial Autonomy to the Country's Federal System. The PPP will take the following measures:

1. The Concurrent Legislative List will be abolished.
2. Provinces will be given their due share in their Natural Resources.
3. Distribution criteria for NFC award will take into account contribution to revenues, geographic size,backwardness and level of development as well as population.
4. The Natural Gas rates and Royalty formula will be as determined by the Constitution of 1973.
5. All Companies engaged in exploration and extraction of Natural Resources will be required to train local people and allocate funds for social development.
6. Provinces will be given part of the sale proceeds in the sale of federal assets in their province.
7. Octroi will revert to local governments and be collected by them.
8. Sales tax will be progressively returned to Provinces.

Local Government

The Pakistan People's Party believes in a three-tier system of Government: Federal, Provincial and Local. Each will enjoy autonomy and function under the law.

The system of Local Government introduced by the military regime, which has been manipulated for political ends, will be revamped to bring it in line with the Party's Devolution Plan.

Primary Education, Basic Health, Water Supply, Sanitation and Population Welfare will be looked after by the Local Governments. The Deputy Commissioner will perform the functions of the DCO. Local Government will be based on modern patterns such as those that exist in the established democracies of the world. Caretaker district governments would be established during elections.

Civil Service Reforms

No modern state can function without an impartial, honest and efficient bureaucracy. The Pakistan People's Party will initiate the implementation of broad-based Civil Service Reforms. Security of service, fixed tenures, merit based appointments, barriers to lateral entry and a ban on inductions from other state institutions are required for an effective bureaucracy. Training of civil servants will be conducted to make the Civil Services citizen-friendly and responsive to the needs and demands of the public.

Police Reforms

The PPP government will embark on a meaningful Police Reforms Programme. The aim of the reforms will to provide security to citizens by creating a crime-free society. The PPP will be tough on crime and the causes of crime. It will foster a professional police force owing allegiance to the Constitution and rule of law, and stop the practice of using the police force for political purposes.

The PPP will expand law enforcement and equip it with modern means to combat crime and maintain security. A strong police force is necessary to combat the forces of internal terrorism.

In the previous PPP Government, Prime Minister Benazir Bhutto instituted a revolutionary programme of Women's Police Stations headed by Women Police Officers to encourage women to report crimes of domestic abuse. This highly successful programme was dismantled by subsequent administrations. It will be immediately reconstituted under the PPP government.

Prison Reforms

The PPP prison reforms aim at reforming prisoners enabling them to integrate into society as responsible citizens. The concept of hard and rigorous labour will be abolished. Prisoners will be encouraged to take classes to learn skills and earn points towards good behaviour early release. They will be paid proper wages for work undertaken and be entitled to purchase facilities for themselves including television, computers and other products. Common rooms will provide Internet access to selected sites as well as reading material in libraries. Medical attention will be given promptly. Proper seating arrangements for interviews will be made.

Prisoners will have the right to make available transport for going to Court hearings in the event of vehicle shortage. Prison administrations will be given rules within which to function and will be autonomous in their functioning. An Ombudsman will be appointed to hear complaints of Prisoners against the violation of jail rules.

Female prisoners will be housed in separate quarters and looked after by female staff. No male staff will be permitted entrance to the female quarters. Female quarters will have similar facilities as male quarters with additional childcare areas.

Rule of Law

The basis of a civilised society lies in the rule of law. In developed countries, those who undermine the majesty of law go to prison. In our country, too often the victims of those who perpetuated injustices are sent to prison. Each elected leader of Pakistan left office brutalized and criminalised while none of the military dictators paid a price even when they disintegrated the nation and mutilated the Constitution.

When the state apparatus perverts the course of justice, evil consequences flow which undermine the premise on which civilised society can be based. The PPP will establish a Truth and Reconciliation Commission to investigate how the so-called National Accountability Bureau tried to pervert the course of justice by torturing witnesses to commit perjury and wasted national resources to politically re-engineer Pakistan.

Judicial Reforms

The Pakistan People's Party is committed to a neutral independent judiciary free of political manipulation. Justice must be fair and blind. From the lower courts to the Supreme Court, the PPP commits its government to a truly independent judiciary.

FATA Reforms

Quaid-e-Awam introduced development for the people of the Federally Administered Tribal Areas and the PPP government headed by Mohtarma Benazir Bhutto continued those policies.

The PPP will restore the authority of the Government in the Tribal Areas and stop the pro-Taliban forces from using its territory to mount attacks on neighbouring Afghanistan. The current situation in the FATA represents a clear danger to national security. The military regime has given up Pakistan's sovereign territory in the Tribal Areas to foreigners. Consequently FATA has become a safe haven for militancy and extremism.

The PPP will reclaim Pakistan's territory and reassert the authority of the government.

The PPP will facilitate the extension of the Laws of Pakistan to FATA, including the Political Parties Act. Mohtarma Benazir Bhutto, Chairperson Pakistan People's Party, has already moved a constitutional petition in the Supreme Court in this regard.

The Party will establish an Elected Council in the Tribal Agencies on the pattern of the Northern Areas to elect local representatives. Development funds will be disbursed through the Elected Agencies Council. The PPP would also establish an independent judicial system in the Tribal Agencies by undoing the present system in which the executive and judicial functions are performed by the same authority.

The PPP will provide the right of Habeus Corpus and establish Sessions Courts in the Tribal Areas. The PPP will enable a right of Appeal to the Peshawar High Court and further to the Supreme Court of Pakistan, providing judicial protection to the people of the FATA.

The seats in the NWFP Provincial Assembly will be enhanced to accommodate representatives from the FATA directly elected by adult franchise, according to the population of each Agency. The PPP will push forward schemes for the educational advancement and economic uplift of FATA, creating job opportunities, increasing quotas in colleges, universities and Government. The tribal people will not be abandoned to the mercy of Political Agents and Maliks.

From centres in the tribal areas, the PPP will provide employment, education and empowerment to the noble Pakhtuns who have lived in hardship.

The PPP will liberate them from backwardness and ignorance.

In order to expedite investment and create jobs, the FATA will be made into a tax-free zone on items manufactured in these areas

Northern Areas

The PPP government will actively pursue policies that promote education, development, and peace in the Northern Areas.

Pakistan and the World

The guiding principles of the Pakistan People's Party shall be the universal principles of peace, reciprocity and flexibility in its foreign relations. The Party is opposed to all forms of terrorism and seeks to build bridges in the world community and promotes inter-faith harmony after the polarities arising from September 11. The Party believes that civilizations and democracies do not go to war, and will not allow extremists to hijack a progressive agenda. The PPP will endeavour to add depth and substance to Pakistan's relations with regional, economic and social organisations. The PPP believes in good neighbourly relations with Afghanistan, India, Iran and the Peoples Republic of China. The Party also believes in further strengthening relations with the USA, Canada, European Union, Japan and the Commonwealth. Pakistan is at the hub of Central Asia, the Gulf and the GCC, hence the PPP will provide a fresh impetus to the trade and cultural ties with these regions. Their special relations with Bangladesh will be strengthened.

Self-Determination

The Pakistan People's Party supports the right of self-determination for all people.

Relations with India

The Simla Agreement of 1973 provides a framework for relations between the two countries. It seeks to reduce tensions with India through peaceful negotiations to outstanding disputes and issues, and recalls the great progress in bilateral relations that took place under the government of Prime Minister Benazir Bhutto. During the December 1988 SAARC Summit, the proposal of Prime Minister Benazir Bhutto to transform SAARC from a cultural organization into an economic one was accepted by the SAARC countries. The PPP government will work for a regional economic framework for the countries of South Asia to benefit all its people through economies of scale. Such a regional economic group has the potential to turn into a global economic powerhouse, attracting investment, creating jobs and eliminating poverty.

Under Mohtarma Benazir Bhutto's governments, the PPP has consistently pushed to replace the infrastructure of conflict with the architecture of peace.

The PPP believes that a prosperous Pakistan is a prosperous South Asia. Maintaining peaceful ties with India is imperative if we wish to achieve these goals. When elected to power, the PPP intends to tackle the social and economic malaise infecting the region by promoting an Asian Common Market that can attract investment, create jobs and build bridges of peace and trade through all of South Asia.

Afghanistan

Military dictators have used Pakistan's proximity to Afghanistan and its strategic importance to the world community to perpetuate dictatorship.

The PPP will not allow Pakistan's territory to be used for cross-border terrorism against Afghanistan. The Party firmly adheres to the principle of non-interference in Afghanistan's internal affairs and favours no group, faction or tribe. The PPP government will engage the Afghan government for an overall understanding on border security, exchange of intelligence, flag meetings between sector commanders, exchange of information, and non-use of force in one another's territories.

The PPP will seek to sign a Treaty of Peace and Cooperation with Afghanistan based on the following principles:

1. Respect for fundamental human rights and for the purposes and principles of the Charter of the United Nations.
2. Settlement of all disputes by peaceful means, such as negotiation, conciliation, arbitration or judicial settlement.
3. Promotion of mutual interests and cooperation.
4. Respect for justice and international obligations.
5. A commitment to the restoration of close cultural, economic and trade ties with Afghanistan
6. The PPP will set up joint working groups with Afghanistan to enhance and rationalize trade between the two nations.
7. The PPP will commit its government to using its resources in Balochistan for the mutual benefit of the energy needs of Afghanistan and Pakistan's largest Province. Terrorism

Terrorism was born in the bowels of dictatorship, which recruited, trained, armed and financed extreme factions while marginalizing the moderate, democratic and pluralistic forces. History teaches us that Democracies do not wage war with each other nor do Democracies promote international terrorism.

The PPP will dismantle militant groups who seek to take hostage the foreign policy of the country and impose their writ through force on the tribal areas of Pakistan and elsewhere.

Distinctions between, and amongst terrorist groups will no longer be maintained.

Defence

The PPP believes that a sound economic base promotes a strong defence. It seeks to identify Pakistan's core defence needs to enable the country to meet its defence targets.

The educational curriculum in defence institutes was prepared to train an officer cadre that could uphold the forces of military rule. That curriculum will be revised to ensure respect for democracy, democratic institutions and elected officials. In addition, all newly appointed Service Chiefs will be given a public oath of office, similar to the one taken at commissioning, prior to their taking up their assignment.

The PPP gave Pakistan a strong defence to safeguard its territorial integrity and national independence. Quaid-e-Awam gave Pakistan the nuclear programme to achieve nuclear parity with India. Mohtarma Benazir Bhutto gave Pakistan missile capability to enable the country to deter aggression.

The PPP will ensure that our armed forces are amongst the best in the world in so that they earn the love and respect of the nation as a Defender of our Motherland free of political involvement and controversy.

Conclusion

The Pakistan People's Party makes a sacred pledge to the people of Pakistan that it will lead our nation to peace and prosperity. It will build a tomorrow better than any of the yesterdays we have known by following in the footsteps of our heroic leaders, Quaid-e-Azam and Quaid-e-Awam to build a federal, democratic, egalitarian Pakistan. The PPP believes that the key to the advancement of Pakistan lies in focusing on employment, education, energy, environment and equality.

From Khyber to Karachi, from the mountains that Alexander the Great crossed to the desert sands of Sindh where Mohammad Bin Qasim brought the Message of Islam, under the banner of Pakistan and the tri-colour flag of Quaid-e-Awam, there will be one nation, one leader, one mission, one programme, one destination, and one voice reflecting the hopes, the desires, the wishes and the aspirations of our great people: *Ilm Roshni, Sab Ko Kaam*

Roti Kapra Aur Makaan Maang Raha Hai Har Insaan

Elections-Speeches & Interviews

Benazir 'waiting for' Musharraf response

PPP Chairperson Benazir Bhutto appears to have softened her attitude towards President Pervez Musharraf following a visit by a top US envoy to Islamabad, which aimed at promoting reconciliation between her and the general.

Although still critical of Gen Musharraf, Ms Bhutto said in an interview to CNN that she was waiting for him to respond to the message Deputy Secretary of State John Negroponte brought from Washington.

Reports in the US media suggest that Mr Negroponte asked both Ms Bhutto and Gen Musharraf to shelve their differences and revive a power-sharing deal.

The US envoy spoke with Ms Bhutto before a 90-minute meeting with Gen Musharraf, which a US official described to The Washington Post as "short of tough love, but still tough"."It was made clear that if things don't change, aid money could be cut, and it was very serious and on the table," the official said. The New York Times noted that Mr Negroponte met Gen Ashfaq Parvez Kayani twice. "The time and attention paid to General Kayani, a pro-Western moderate, seemed to signal American support for him," the newspaper said.

In her interview to CNN Late Edition, Ms Bhutto twice avoided criticising Gen Musharraf when asked to do so, telling the interviewer instead: "I know where you want to take me."

The interviewer also played the tape of an earlier interview with Gen Musharraf who accused Ms Bhutto of using his conciliatory gesture to come to Pakistan and later taking a confrontational stance against him. The interviewer then asked her if she still wanted to send him a reconciliatory message.

Ms Bhutto, who usually uses such opportunities to hit back with full force, politely said: "If Gen Musharraf is not responding to Washington's call to retire (as chief of army staff), and Washington is giving him $10 billion, I wonder he would be ever ready to respond to my call for a political reconciliation.

She said she had made a reconciliatory arrangement with Gen Musharraf to "avoid the mess we are in today." But when Gen Musharraf suspended the Constitution she came to the conclusion that he was not interested in giving the opposition a fair chance.

When the interviewer asked if she was going to reconsider her decision now, Ms Bhutto said: "I know where you are taking me. Let's first see if he responds to Washington."

She said for holding fair and free elections, Gen Musharraf needed to reconstruct the Election Commission, suspend existing nazims who could manipulate the elections and take other steps.

Gen Musharraf, she said, also needed to send a powerful message to the militants that they could not get away with attacking politicians by calling in international investigators to probe the attack on her procession.

Ms Bhutto said the government's decision to release her and other political prisoners was timed to coincide with Mr Negroponte's visit to send a positive signal to Washington.

Several thousand political workers, however, were still behind bars, she added.

Ms Bhutto said the US envoy did the right thing in publicly asking the Musharraf government to lift the curbs on the media, release political workers and retire as COAS.

The nation, she said, was waiting for Gen Musharraf to give a fixed date to retire as army chief but he had not done so.

Ms Bhutto also responded to former US Secretary of Madeleine Albright's recent statement that as bad as Gen Musharraf might be, he had made a major contribution to fighting terrorism.

Ms Bhutto said what the general had done was not enough as terrorists were spreading their tentacles from the tribal to settled areas of the NWFP and were also knocking at the doors of Islamabad.

She said that in Swat the government was conducting carpet-bombing which was also killing innocent civilians.

Ms Bhutto said she would like to see the local population co-opted against the terrorists.

Musharraf's Electoral Farce

By Benazir Bhutto

All through the years of the Soviet empire, its Politburo held "elections." Of course, calling something an election and actually having it be an election are different things.

I am under house arrest in Lahore, barricaded in by Pakistani police with bayonets. Despite Gen. Pervez Musharraf's announcement of a date for parliamentary elections, I doubt that we are in for a change. I cautioned the general earlier this year that his election as president by the present parliament was illegal. He insisted otherwise.

They agreed to disagree and decided that we both would accept a ruling by the Supreme Court regarding eligibility. Yet when the court was on the brink of deciding, Musharraf imposed martial law by suspending the constitution, and he removed several of the Supreme Court justices.

Today the nation is paying for his mistake.

They are witnessing a farce in Pakistan: While an election schedule has been announced, the problem lies in what has not been announced. No indication has been given as to whether Musharraf will keep his previous commitment to retire as army chief.

No date has been given for the lifting of emergency rule; the reconstitution of the election commission; the implementation of fair election practices; the removal of biased officials; or the suspension of the mayors, who control the guns and the funds — that is, police and government resources to adversely influence elections.

Moreover, judges, lawyers, human rights activists and students across the country are in prison or under house arrest. The independent media have been shut down, television stations stopped from broadcasting news.

Several foreign journalists have been expelled. Thousands of political activists, a majority from my Pakistan People's Party, have been arrested.

Police have erected barricades and deployed armored personnel carriers and trucks filled with sand to cut off access to my house and to prevent people from going from one city to another. Musharraf knows how to crack down against pro-democracy forces. He is, however, unwilling or unable to track down and arrest Osama bin Laden or contain the extremists. This is the reality of Pakistan in November 2007.

The only terror that Musharraf's regime seems able to confront is the terror of his own illegitimacy. This is the second time Musharraf has imposed martial law and the second time he has sacked judges since taking over the country in a coup in 1999. It was then that he first promised "to bring true democracy."

The election commission has promulgated election rolls judged illegitimate by Pakistan's Supreme Court and the National Democratic Institute for International Affairs. Some polling sites have been kept secret. Musharraf's political opposition is banned from campaigning or organizing and has been denied access to state-controlled media. They cannot meet, we cannot rally, and when we try to bring the people to the streets they are gassed, beaten and shot at with rubber bullets. This is not only a military dictatorship, it is a classic police state.

On top of a litany of assaults on the rule of law, the General has unilaterally amended the Army Act of 1952 to grant the army the power to try civilians in military courts. Courts-martial will operate by military rules in secret, and defendants are not allowed legal representation.

No attempt has been made to differentiate between average citizens and terrorism suspects associated with militant groups. Many believe that these laws were passed to intimidate pro-democracy forces, not to try terrorism suspects. This is the "democracy" that Musharraf envisages.

While living in America when I attended Harvard in the early 1970s, I saw for myself the awesome, almost miraculous, power of a people to change policy through democratic means. Today I am seeing the power of the people coalescing once again. Journalists, judges, and political and civil activists have joined together against Musharraf's second declaration of martial law. They see him as the obstacle to the democratization of Pakistan.

This is why, I have called upon Gen. Musharraf to resign as President and Chief of Army Staff, and to pave the way for the composition of an interim government of national consensus that will oversee the transfer of power to duly elected representatives of the people.

The people of the Soviet Union knew that "elections" for the Politburo were fraudulent. The people of Pakistan know that elections under martial law are a similar sham.

The Present Unrest in Pakistan

By Benazir Bhutto & David Miliband

And we're going straight to Pakistan, to Lahore, where we can talk to Benazir Bhutto who is surrounded by thousands of troops and being prevented from having her march and who is on the line. Good morning.

Benazir Bhutto: Good morning.

JN: What is the situation where you now find yourself?

BB: Well we've got about four thousand policemen all around the house including in the neighbours, armoured personnel carriers and massive trucks filled with red sand, barbed wire, and I'm just wondering when we have this huge deployment where Police of this kind can't be used to hunt down Osama bin Laden.

The whole problem in Pakistan has been the inability of General Musharraf 's regime to focus on the real threat which is coming from the extremists in the tribal areas of Pakistan and instead they've concentrated on marginalizing the moderate forces which has just fuelled extremism further.

JN: For some time you've been engaged in, a kind of dialogue with General Musharraf. What is your view now of his hold on power?

BB: Well I think General Musharraf should be, if he's lost the confidence of the people of Pakistan, he's at war with the judiciary of the country having arrested the judges, he's taken on the Bar Association, imposed censorship and basically alienated the press and the nation. He's attacked NGO groups who are also protesting, he is unable to give the nation a fair election, he's announced an election date no doubt, but one should look at all the things he didn't announce. He was given good advice by the Commonwealth, by the Foreign Secretary, by President Bush's Administration but he doesn't listen to the advice he is given, he is bent on maintaining and sustaining a dictatorship and dictatorship and Pakistan simply don't go together. It's dictatorship that has led to the political protest, it's dictatorship which has led to the rise of extremism.

JN: Can we take it from what you've just said that there are no circumstances under which you would serve in power with General Musharraf now?

BB: That's right there are no circumstances in which I could see myself serving with General Musharraf. I tried for more than a year, I did my best, I worked out a roadmap for democracy but he went back on that and imposed martial law. After that there were several people, foreign countries and people inside, that publicly called, and Foreign Secretary Miliband, that rightly called for General Musharraf to give a date when he would hold general election, give a date for when he would retire as Chief of Army Staff, release the judges and the political prisoners and lift the gags on the media.

Now these were given by a friend of Pakistan and would have helped diffuse the internal situation. But ...

JN: Well ...

BB: ... unfortunately General Musharraf did too little and if he does anything now it will be too late. He's alienated the people with his brute force by breaking in to homes, his police have broken in to homes, so I really think it's impossible for the People's Party and myself to work with him any more.

JN: They'll be talking to the Foreign Secretary in a moment, in fact I think he's listening to what you're saying now. Given what you've just said what would you like him to do and the British Government to do?

BB: Well, it might not be very diplomatic but I would like to say to the Foreign Secretary to ask General Musharraf to step down. And certainly I feel that as long as General Musharraf is there the turmoil in Pakistan will continue and Britain really needs to look at the situation whether a nuclear armed nation, a country like Pakistan, can afford.

JN: Well ...

BB: ... to go under. It's imploding. Britain has interests.

JN: ... we'll ask ...

BB: ... in, in the region and it, we see our tribal areas have become safe havens for extremists ...

JN: ... what will you ...

BB: ... (indistinct) NATO troops and attack people in Pakistan.

JN: Finally, and briefly if you can Miss Bhutto, what will you do now?

BB: Well I intend to continue marching for democracy I intend to continue marching for an end to martial law.

JN: Benazir Bhutto in Lahore thank you.

Sarah Montague: Well with the time at ten minutes to eight we are now joined by the Foreign Secretary David Miliband who was listening to Benazir Bhutto there. Good morning.

David Miliband: Good morning.

SM: Will you ask President Musharraf to step down?

DB: Well we've been absolutely clear already that it's vital that President Musharraf fulfils his commitment to step down as head of the Army, that's one of the four pieces of the international jigsaw that have been absolutely a point of consensus and obviously I've talked about those points with Benazir Bhutto on two occasions on the phone and also in person. Stepping down as head of the Army is, is key, free and fair elections vital, media restrictions lifted and obviously the political prisoners, many of them from Benazir Bhutto's party, also have to be released.

SM: But as you will have heard her saying there whatever he does now it is too late so will you ask him to step down?

DB: Well we, we've made clear that he does have to step down as head of the Army and that democratic forces have to have their sway in.

SM: Mr Miliband forgive me for pushing you but did, she's specifically saying that you need to ask him to step down as President.

DB: Right well that's the first time I've heard her say that, I, I, I came ir. halfway through the interview.

SM: I think it is the first time that she's said it or at least ...

DB: ... yeah.

SM: ... within the last hour ...

DB: ... yeah, I, I, I ...

SM: ... what is your response to it?

DB: ... well I think that the, as I said in the House of Commons last week, the situation in Pakistan is moving very fast. Even in the last twenty four hours we've had the meeting of the Commonwealth Ministers' Action Group which is saying that unless the situation improves then Pakistan will be suspended from the Commonwealth. I will look at, obviously, at what Benazir Bhutto has said but the, the point of consensus up to now with all of our international partners and I have to say also with opposition figures within Pakistan has been about the centrality of free and fair elections because in the end it has to be the people of Pakistan who decide who their Government should be, not me.

SM: Her argument though, as I say, is that it's too late for him to do something now, it's too late, there's nothing he can do, he needs to step down. From what you're saying, it's not too late.

DB: Well I think that's a matter in the end for the constitution of Pakistan. There, there is a constitution in Pakistan, it needs to be respected, it's vital that at the heart are free and fair elections.

SM: But it's not, forgive me, it's not being respected at the moment is it?

DB: ... well it's not being respected, it's been suspended as, there, there's an emergency rule there, the constitution has been suspended. Elections have been confirmed for, for, before the 9th of January but as I said in the House of Commons in the Foreign Affairs Debate yesterday we must make sure that the elections are free and fair in that the opposition have a proper chance to put their case, they'll, the electoral rolls are in a proper state, and obviously also that political prisoners are released. So it's got to be the reality and substance of proper elections, not just the words of them.

SM: So the British Government position is the same as the Commonwealth, the, the, made yesterday, that within ten days the military rule must be lifted?

DB: Abs, absolutely the, the Commonwealth position was one that UK played an important part in creating. The importance of ten days, just for the benefit of listeners, is that the Commonwealth Heads of Government will be meeting next week, at the end of next week, in Kampala, and the 22nd of November relates to, to that meeting and that's, that's why the ten days has become important.

SM: You were invited on to speak before, of course, the development in Pakistan on the comments made by the Prime Minister last night who talked about foreign policy saying his foreign policy, he described it as hard headed internationalism, Now you, of course, as Foreign Secretary are the man implementing that policy, what does it mean to you?

DB: I think that the most important thing that it means is that we will use all the tools at our disposal, the so called soft power of diplomacy and trade but also the hard power of our military forces who are in action around the world, to ensure that we can advance British values and interests, and the more we can do that in international institutions obviously the more effective we are at utilising the relationships that we, and partnerships that we have around the world.

And I think one of the lessons of the, of the period since the end of the Cold War, the lessons of the period since September 2001, is that, you know, in a way Pakistan makes this point, if you pose the choice as either you favour democracy or you favour security, in other words either you favour aid programmes or you favour military action, you don't get it right. You have to use both and whether it be in Darfur, which the Prime Minister talked about yesterday, we've got to make sure that we get our programmes for economic governance, for political reform and for security right. I think that's the heart of the message the Prime Minister was putting across.

Bhutto: Time for Musharraf to go

By Benazir Bhutto

Bhutto says she has been placed under house arrest for seven days. Protesters open fire on two police stations in

Karachi, AP reports Bhutto says she would prefer to live in a Pakistani jail than forced to leave. Bhutto says talks on power-sharing deal with Musharraf have been shelved. Former Pakistan Prime Minister Benazir Bhutto called on President Gen. Pervez Musharraf to immediately step down in the wake of a mass crackdown on the opposition.

Protesters in Karachi meanwhile have reportedly opened fire on two police stations in protest as Bhutto remained under house arrest in Lahore, according to The Associated Press.

"It's time for him to leave," said Bhutto in a phone interview with CNN Tuesday morning, as Pakistani riot police arrested her supporters.

It marked the first time she has called on Musharraf, who is both President and Army Chief, to completely give up power. In the past, she has called on him to renounce his military role while serving as President.

Bhutto said while she has tried to work with Musharraf on a "roadmap to democracy," the arrests of thousands of people convinced her he must go.

Musharraf declared a state of emergency and suspended democracy.

"There's a total trust deficit," Bhutto said, confirming that she has been placed under house arrest for seven days. Watch what else emerged from her interview »

In her CNN interview, she also addressed media reports that Musharraf may have her deported.

"I'm told by Sky television that the regime is getting a C-130 military aircraft ready to take me away, presumably to my home in Karachi. But I have not been given any indication of whether I will be taken out of this house arrest or whether I will be taken to my own house or to any unknown destination," Bhutto said.

"So I'm totally in the dark at this moment on what this regime is planning to do with me."

Asked if she would leave the country if the government tries to force her out, Bhutto replied, "No, I won't go. Pakistan is my country.

"I belong to Pakistan and I cannot be banished. I would prefer to live in a Pakistani jail than to be forced to leave."

While authorities barricaded the streets surrounding the house where she is staying, only a "handful" of officials and members of Bhutto's Pakistan People's Party (PPP) had tried to breach the cordon, CNN's Karl Penhaul reported.

"These party officials show up to the barricades. They symbolically chant two or three slogans and then almost voluntarily they seem to be stepping into police vans to be taken off for some kind of arrest," Penhaul reported.

"But certainly, there is no massing of party interests here and certainly, right now, there are many more police and, indeed, many more TV cameras than there are supporters of Benazir Bhutto."

Opposition groups had hoped to stage a five-day Lahore-to-Islamabad march and were counting on a groundswell of popular support to carry out the protest, but there appeared to be none.

Police and opposition officials reported the scattered burning of tires in Lahore to protest the barricades.

Meanwhile, several hundred police officers surrounded the house where Bhutto was staying and declared it a "subjail," sending jail staff to monitor the situation.

Bhutto was briefly confined to her villa compound in Islamabad in an effort to halt a massive opposition protest in Rawalpindi against Musharraf's November 3 declaration of emergency rule.

He has called it necessary to crack down on Islamic terrorists massing strength in volatile tribal regions along the Afghan border.

The opposition says the emergency order amounts to martial law and amounts to a power grab by Musharraf.

Pakistani authorities have shut down media outlets and jailed opposition leaders and lawyers who protested Musharraf's sacking of a number of Supreme Court justices, including Chief Justice Ikhtar Muhammed Chaudhry.

Opposition leaders contend Musharraf's emergency order was issued to avoid what they said was the top court's impending decision that would have nullified his recent election victory on grounds he was ineligible.

Musharraf has said the newly installed court judges "accept the election," and he repeated his vow to step down as military chief as soon as the court approves his third term.

Musharraf announced that a parliamentary vote would take place before January 9, adding that it could take place with the state of emergency still in effect. In fact, he said, the emergency order "will ensure absolutely fair and transparent elections."

In the wake of the emergency order and crackdown, Bhutto has said talks on a power-sharing deal with Musharraf have been shelved. Fellow opposition leaders have criticized her for considering such a deal.

The United States and Britain, among other nations, have cautiously urged Musharraf to rescind the emergency decree.

Senior State Department officials told CNN Tuesday that Deputy Security of State John Negroponte was expected in the Pakistani capital of Islamabad for talks later this week with Musharraf.

Negroponte is expected to pressure Musharraf to end the emergency rule, shed his role as the country's military leader and stick to his calls for elections in early January, the officials said.

Embassy spokeswoman Liz Colton said Negroponte had long been scheduled to visit Pakistan as part of a strategic dialogue between the two countries.

Those talks were to include the war on terror, but Colton said that given the state of emergency imposed by Pakistan, that would be the focus of the talks.

Meanwhile, the Commonwealth, a 53-nation alliance, made up largely of former members of the British Empire, declared that Musharraf's emergency decree was taken "outside the provisions of the Constitution."

The group demanded that the Pakistani leader rescind the decree, step down as military chief, release those detained under the emergency decree, remove restrictions on the press and hold elections as called for in the constitution.

"If, after review of progress, Pakistan has failed to implement these necessary measures, we will suspend Pakistan from the councils of the Commonwealth," said Commonwealth Secretary-General Don McKinnon, in anticipating the next November 22 meeting.

Benazir Bhutto Tests Pervez Musharraf's Strength

By Christina Lamb and Dean Nelson in Islamabad

BENAZIR BHUTTO last night demanded that General Pervez Musharraf step down and insisted that any hope of an understanding with him was now "finished".

"By suspending the constitution and declaring a state of emergency he reneged on his promises to us," Pakistan's former prime minister declared. "Any understanding between us is now finished."

In a late night telephone interview with The Sunday Times, Bhutto sounded tired but elated after what she described as "another long day". She spoke of her outrage at Musharraf's acts of the past week that have plunged the country into crisis.

"I feel absolutely shocked that we have these year-long negotiations and we agree to work together, then he turns around and suspends the constitution," she said. "I have to wonder if he was ever serious.

"It wasn't as if he had no alternative. Why did he do this when he could have carried on with the road map towards democracy agreed with the country's biggest political party?"

His actions, Bhutto said, had forced her to call people out into the streets, something she had been eager to avoid for fear of bloodshed. It was to prevent this, she said, that she had agreed the deal which saw him dropping corruption charges against her, enabling her to return home last month after 8 years in exile.

"Now he's left us no choice but to call out the people," she said. "I face a difficult predicament. I've long been worried about creeping Talibanisation in Pakistan and if I don't take the lead then there may well be extremist elements that take advantage. So I have no choice."

Bhutto insisted that the only way to avoid violence is for Musharraf to step down. "He's put himself into a corner and it's of his own making," she said.

"His two trump cards were the international community and the army. Now he's losing both. The only option he has is to step aside and hand power to an interim government of national consensus that will oversee elections. His time is up."

Under international pressure, Musharraf announced that he would hold elections by February 15. Malik Mohammed Qayyum, the attorney-general, told reporters that the state of emergency would "end within one month". But Bhutto dismissed these assurances. "It would be impossible to have elections in these circumstances where both the courts and the election commission are in his control," she said.

Musharraf 's declaration of what amounted to martial law, arresting thousands, locking up judges and taking television stations off the air, has seen Bhutto transformed from someone doing a deal with a dictator into a woman and mother prepared to sacrifice everything for democracy.

She vowed to go ahead with the three-day Long March planned for this week from Lahore to Islamabad, despite further warnings of assassination attempts such as the suicide bombs that killed 140 people during her return to Karachi three weeks ago. The march will bring her into all-out confrontation with the regime.

"I know there are risks for my personal safety but I have to look at the bigger picture," she said.

"Pakistan is facing the threat of disintegration. One by one the tribal areas have fallen to [the] Taliban and now they are advancing further into the northwest frontier. With an unrepresentative government and an army that is leaderless and rudderless, Pakistan is facing its most serious threat since 1971 [when the country split into two]."

However, the government insisted that the march would be blocked. "All marches, processions and political gatherings are banned at the moment, so I'm afraid the march has been outlawed," said Tariq Azim, the information minister who was once an ally of Bhutto.

"They are committed to upholding the law and it must be applied equally for everyone, including Benazir Bhutto."

Bhutto said she would not be deterred. "Even if they block it, it's like a strike call because it paralyses the whole area. Either way they lose and we win. If they don't interrupt it we show the numbers we can get out. If they do bring out all those police and teargassing, it still brings everything to a standstill and shows the numbers we would have had."

Bhutto was speaking from her home in Islamabad after spending the day building up pressure on Musharraf with a series of high-profile visits around the Pakistani capital, constantly trailed by the microphones and lenses of the international media.

First she met non-governmental organisations and local journalists banned from reporting current events and protesting against new laws which impose jail sentences on anyone who criticises Musharraf. She also kept up international pressure on the government by holding a meeting with diplomats last night.

For the most part Bhutto seemed able to move unimpeded. The freedom of movement she is enjoying, while authorities admit that they have arrested more than 3,000 people, had prompted speculation that she might still be in negotiations with Musharraf.

However, Bhutto insisted that there is no contact between the two sides and that it is because of her high international profile that Musharraf has not arrested her. "The international interest in Pakistan is giving me more security, although at the same time it's made me a bigger target for assassins," she said.

It is increasingly hard to see a way out for Musharraf. Bhutto's call for millions to join the march has alarmed senior military officers. It is widely believed that General Ashfaq Parvez Kayani, Musharraf's deputy chief of army staff, is unhappy about the emergency. He is being touted as the man to topple Musharraf and hand the government back to civilian politicians.

"Musharraf is making one bad decision after another," said Bhutto. "First there were the peace agreements with the Taliban in the tribal areas, then the dismissal of the chief justice now all this is coming home to roost. The only answer is for him to move aside."

The last time Bhutto announced a Long March in 1993, against the government of Nawaz Sharif and Ghulam Ishaq Khan, then President she never needed to take a step. The night before the march, Khan resigned and called elections.

"That would be nice," she said last night.

Musharraf's Martial Plan

By Benazir Bhutto

NOV. 3, 2007, will be remembered as the blackest day in the history of Pakistan. Let us be perfectly clear: Pakistan is a military dictatorship. Last Saturday, Gen. Pervez Musharraf removed all pretense of a transition to democracy by conducting what was in effect yet another extra constitutional coup.

In doing so he endangered the viability of Pakistan as an independent state. He presented the country's democratic forces with a tough decision acquiesce to the brutality of the dictatorship or take over the streets and show the world where the people of Pakistan really stand.

General Musharraf also presented the democratic world and especially the countries of the West with a question. Will they back up their democratic rhetoric with concrete action, or will they once again back down in the face of his bluff?

In my view, General Musharraf's ruling party understood that it would be trounced in any free elections and, together with its allies within the intelligence services, contrived to have the Constitution suspended and elections indefinitely postponed. Very conveniently, the assassination attempt against me last month that resulted in the deaths of at least 140 people is being used as the rationale to stop the democratic process by which my party would most likely have swept parliamentary elections. Maybe this explains why the government refuses to allow the F.B.I. and Scotland Yard to assist in a forensic investigation of the bombings.

As I write, demonstrations are taking place across Pakistan. Opposition party members, lawyers, judges, human rights advocates and journalists have been rounded up by the police without charge. The press has been seriously constrained. The chief justice of the Supreme Court and many other judges are believed to be under house arrest.

The United States, Britain and much of the West have always said the right things about democracy in Pakistan and around the world. I recall the words of President Bush in his second inaugural address when he said: "All who live in tyranny and hopelessness can know: the United States will not ignore your oppression, or excuse your oppressors. When you stand for your liberty, we will stand with you."

The United States alone has given the Musharraf government more than $10 billion in aid since 2001. They do not know exactly where or how this money has been spent, but it is clear that it has not brought about the defeat of the Taliban and Al Qaeda, nor succeeded in capturing Osama bin Laden, nor has it broken the opium trade. It certainly has not succeeded in improving the quality of life of the children and families of Pakistan.

The United States can promote democracy which is the only way to truly contain extremism and terrorism by telling General Musharraf that it does not accept martial law, and that it expects him to conduct free, fair, impartial and internationally monitored elections within 60 days under a reconstituted election commission. He should be given that choice: democracy or dictatorship with isolation.

While the world must do its part to confront tyranny, the primary responsibility rests in the hands of the people of Pakistan. It is incumbent on Pakistanis to tell General Musharraf that martial law will not stand. The overwhelming majority of Pakistanis are moderate; it is my hope that they will unite in a coalition of moderation to marginalize both the dictators and the extremists, to restore civilian rule to the presidency and to shut down political madrassas, the Islamic schools that stock weapons and preach violence.

It is dangerous to stand up to a military dictatorship, but more dangerous not to. The moment has come for the Western democracies to show us in their actions, and not just in their rhetoric, which side they are on. Benazir Bhutto, the prime minister of Pakistan from 1988 to 1990 and from 1993 to 1996, is the leader of the Pakistan People's Party.

Bhutto to Musharraf: They Can Still Deal

By Aryn Baker

As police and the military used tear gas to suppress a protest by thousands of lawyers in Pakistan's largest cities, opposition leader Benazir Bhutto spoke to TIME about the imposition of martial law by President Pervez Musharraf. She said that Musharraf was falling under the sway of the more radical parts of his Pakistan Muslim League (Q) (PML-Q) party. Still, she said she was not shutting the door on negotiations with Musharraf. Bhutto, who leads the huge People's Party, has not asked her millions of fervent followers to come out into the streets. During the interview, she evinced some sympathy for Musharraf over his feud with the Supreme Court. The court was about to decide whether he could simultaneously lead the military and be President when martial law was declared and the chief justice put under house arrest. The same Supreme Court was also to decide on the merits of Musharraf's U.S.-backed deal with Bhutto to drop corruption charges against her and her husband Asif Zardari so she could return from exile to run for office and regain the Prime Ministership. Nevertheless, Bhutto said that "extra-constitutional" methods were unnecessary and that martial law will only exacerbate Islamic militancy and terrorism. Meanwhile, the capital of Islamabad was in lockdown, with no demonstrations in sight as the roads surrounding the Supreme Court building were blocked by tanks and barbed wire and lined with hundreds of security personnel.

TIME: What do you make of Musharraf's declaration of emergency?

BENAZIR BHUTTO: Actually, we call it martial law. The constitution has been suspended and while Musharraf is terming it an emergency for international consumption, he has actually in his capacity of Chief of Army Staff suspended the constitution of Pakistan and promulgated a new provisional order. The result of this is that he has stopped democracy in its tracks. And he has given an extended life to his ruling PML-Q party.

I may mention that the PML-Q has some moderate elements in it, but the core strength of the Q comes from those people associated with General Zia ul Haq the military dictator of the '80s that established the mujheddin and it is these people whose governance has seen, by coincidence or otherwise, the growth of [Islamic] militancy in Pakistan. They are the ones that have presided over the signing of peace treaties and cease-fires in the tribal areas. They have lost control of our tribal areas.

The militants are knocking on the doors of Swat; they are eyeing the capital city of Islamabad. They have access to superior sources of plastic explosives and they have constructed bombs and improvised explosive devices to be used against my rally, against the ISI [Inter-Services Intelligence] bus [in Rawalpindi on Oct. 20], against officers, against the air force. They call it suicide bombing, but it is not suicide bombing. Their analysis is that these are IEDs [Improvised Explosive Devices] that are being placed and have been hushed up under the name of suicide bombings.

That's why we have requested international assistance on the inquiry of the bomb blasts that took place on my procession on October 19th, because it follows the same pattern. And we think intelligence cooperation should be between Pakistani police and international police agencies, Scotland Yard or the FBI. They want to get to the bottom of the culprits behind these blasts.

And what does this mean for the future of the country?

It is a very big problem. It means that dictatorship will be sustained until it is reversed. It is a clear breach of the understanding that Musharraf has with my party. They have been engaged with him for a period of time for a negotiated peaceful transfer to democracy. He has promised to retire as army chief. He has promised to hold fair elections, and implement fair election reform. Contrary to these promises, he has imposed emergency without consulting me. They advised him against doing this. And he chose to side with the hard-core elements of the ruling PML-Q. Now I feel that until democracy is restored we will be fueling the forces of extremism.

Does this mean that all negotiations with him are off? Are you pulling the plug?

They are not pulling any plug; he is the one that stopped negotiating once I returned to the country. He calls me up to condole, and then after that I heard that his people were going to come and visit me to talk about the second phase, which was the implementation of the fair election proposal followed by the balance of power between the presidency and the parliament. But they never came. They kept saying they would come, but they never did. They never showed up. So in fact they just bought time, and then suddenly when I was in Dubai they announced martial law. I caught the first plane back to be with my people who have suffered so much. My people who had sacrificed 158 lives — the final death toll of the Karachi blasts.

So what does this mean for negotiations? Are you done?

Well, he may break his word, but we don't. They keep our word; we keep our commitments. They went forward with the process that we thought was in the national interest. Which was to take this nuclear armed nation, which is a key country in this region, towards democracy, so that there would be stability so that we could unite the forces of moderation, so we could confront the forces of extremism. But unilaterally they broke the negotiations by the imposition of emergency. So now we are demanding a return to the constitution, Musharraf to retire as chief of army staff, and that he hold the elections on time as he earlier committed to us.

They told him in August during our talks in London, that there were issues with his eligibility and that he needed to have constitutional reforms like balance of power between the presidency and the parliament. That could help the country go through this period with stability. But he said no, "I am eligible." This martial law was imposed because he was expecting an adverse court order on his eligibility. Whereas the eligibility issue could have been settled by parliament if he was willing to pay the political price that we demanded. But he preferred to impose martial law over seeking a political solution. And that's the dangerous part, that's the part that worries me.

If he goes ahead and answers your demands, do you think you can work with him in good faith?

My faith has certainly been shaken, but I would ask what's the timetable? As we have seen, the promises are made but then they are broken. What we are talking about to restore good faith is up-front action. They are talking about up-front revival of the constitution, up-front retirement as chief of army staff and up-front elections on schedule, announced by November 15th, and held by January 15th. If he is prepared to take these measures, along with some others, then we can say that all that has occurred, we will let it drop. But if he is not prepared to do this, then it becomes very difficult to work with someone who makes a promise but cannot keep it.

And what about reinstating the Supreme Court?

Well, we think that the judiciary should be respected.

So would you want to see the reinstatement of Supreme Court Chief Justice Iftikhar Chaudhry? And all the other dismissed judges?

Well, if there is a complaint against the judges, the government should follow the normal avenues of complaint.

There are normal ways to address complaints against judges. You don't need extra-constitutional measures.

Do you think these judges were actually in the wrong?

I am not aware of the details but I know that General Musharraf has made some allegations against the judges, and they are allegations that they must respond to. They are very serious allegations. Without going into the merits of the allegations, I'm simply saying that there are ways to deal with these allegations of misconduct and not use them as a pretext for the imposition of martial law.

When Musharraf made his declaration of emergency rule, he said it was in the interest of fighting terrorism in Pakistan. Do you agree with him?

I agree that there is terrorism in the country, I believe it has spread since the 2002 elections when the People's Party was excluded from the government, but I don't believe martial law was declared to stop terrorism, I believe it was declared to stop an adverse decision by the Supreme Court on Musharraf's eligibility to remain as President and to keep the ruling PML-Q in power.

What kind of effect do you think martial law will have on terrorism?

This will worsen the situation for terrorism. It will take the focus of the army and the police away from fighting terrorists. The militants and terrorists would have wanted nothing better than a fresh confrontation between the people and the government. And it is to prevent instability that my party and I have taken the decision to have political negotiations with General Musharraf in order to weaken the terrorists. But I am afraid his actions have played into the terrorist's hands. And he should remedy it. All of us who have a stake in eliminating terrorism must all work together to reverse what has happened.

Don't expect the Constitution to be restored before a year

By Benazir Bhutto

- Urges global community to convince Gen Musharraf to restore Constitution

- Says suspension of fundamental rights hampering protest efforts

NBC News' Andrea Mitchell spoke with former premier Benazir Bhutto at her home in Karachi. Bhutto had just arrived in Pakistan after the imposition of a state of emergency by President Pervez Musharraf.

MITCHELL: Prime Minister Bhutto, tell me what your latest information is about what President Musharraf has done, and your reaction to it.

BHUTTO: General Musharraf has suspended the Constitution of Pakistan, so it's really a declaration of martial law. But he's calling it an emergency. An emergency sounds more palatable to international opinion. But the proclamation says that the Constitution of the Islamic Republic of Pakistan shall remain in abeyance, and that's very worrying. My party and I would like to see the Constitution restored.

MITCHELL: Is there any justification that you know of for him declaring this suspension of the Constitution?

BHUTTO: Well, General Musharraf has tried to justify the imposition of martial law or emergency claiming that there has been an ascendancy in the activities of extremists. I agree with him that there has been ascendancy in the activities of the extremists, but I don't believe in the solution. In my view, dictatorship fuels extremism. The extremists feed off dictatorship, and dictatorship feeds off the extremists. The dictatorship needs the extremists to justify its existence, and the extremists need dictatorship to expand and spread. So I believe the solution lies in respecting the Constitution, respecting the rule of law, and investing in the people, trusting the people, and allowing the people to determine their future.

MITCHELL: What are you planning to do?

BHUTTO: I returned to Pakistan to give moral support to the people of my country and to tell them that they were not alone in the struggle for the restoration of our Constitution. I plan to meet with leaders of other political parties and discuss with them the policies we should make in trying to seek a restoration of our Constitution.

MITCHELL: At this point, given what General Musharraf has done, have you abandoned any plan to work out a political agreement where you would run, and become prime minister, and work with him in a government?

BHUTTO: Well, it's very difficult for me to work with a military leader. General Musharraf has committed to the Supreme Court of Pakistan, and he has personally assured me that he would retire as chief of Army Staff. But now he has declared martial law in this capacity, as chief of Army Staff. The Constitution gives our president emergency powers, but the constitutional articles for emergency have not been utilised. Instead, General Musharraf has said that in his capacity, that "I, General Pervez Musharraf, chief of the Army Staff, proclaim emergency". So, he has actually said that he will continue as chief of Army Staff, and that makes for a very difficult situation. Of course, if he was to restore the Constitution and retire as chief of Army Staff, that would be a totally different situation. It would lend confidence that he was once again considering the democratic route. But not while he remains chief of Army Staff and suspends the Constitution.

MITCHELL: And what do you think you and your supporters can do now, politically or in any other fashion?

BHUTTO: Well, we would like to protest the imposition of martial law, and we would like to raise our voices for the restoration of democracy. So we're going to be meeting together to discuss the most effective ways of doing that. They are calling upon the international community to use its enormous leverage with General Musharraf to persuade him that this is a regressive step, it's a violation of the promises and the commitments that he made to the people of Pakistan and to the international community. And that if he really wishes to fight extremists, then the best way to do that is to trust the people, restore the Constitution, establish an independent Election Commission, and hold fair, free and impartial elections.

MITCHELL: Have you had any communication with Secretary Rice or any American officials?

BHUTTO: Not yet. I just came to Pakistan. But before, earlier, yesterday I heard that there were efforts being made to stop the imposition of emergency. And I also planned to come back to Pakistan so that I could also contact the people in the regime here and tell them not to take this step. But by the time I left, they had already taken this step.

MITCHELL: I've seen a report from Sky News that you believe that this is an attempt to delay elections for a year or two. Is that what you believe is happening?

BHUTTO: That's right. My reports from inside the regime are that there is going to be a salami (piecemeal) approach, where we are going to be told this is a temporary measure for three to six months, and then it will be extended for another six months. And in fact, I believe that the hard-liners within the regime, and there are many hard-liners which served with an earlier military dictator of the 80's, who formed the Afghan muhjahideen who went on to become Al Qaeda and the Taliban. These hard-liners believe that America will be caught up in the presidential elections for a year. And then a new administration in the US will take another year to settle down. And they feel they need two years to drive NATO out of Afghanistan, destabilise (Afghan President) Karzai, and set up a kind of puppet government there, as well to expand their influence in Pakistan. These are the reports I'm getting from inside the regime.

MITCHELL: You think that General Musharraf is trying to suspend the Constitution for an extended period of time, for a matter of years?

BHUTTO: Yes. But he will not say so immediately. It will be done in installments. I believe this position has been taken to suspend the Constitution for at least one year, if not two.

MITCHELL: I was going to ask you if you're concerned for your safety?

BHUTTO: I do have concerns for the safety of all the people of my country, not just myself. I am unsure what will happen; this is a difficult period, but at the same time, General Musharraf has also been sensitive to international opinion. He was going to impose emergency earlier, and then the United States intervened; there was a long conversation with the secretary of State. And so I do believe that it's very important for us to try and get Pakistan back on to the democratic track. To persuade General Musharraf to restore the Constitution, and to respect the courts, to respect the judiciary, and to trust the people of the country.

MITCHELL: Prime Minister, what would you like the United States government to do at this stage?

BHUTTO: I would like the United States government to telephone General Musharraf to tell him that it's not possible for them to support the suspension of Pakistan's Constitution or the sacking of the judges. And that democracy is important, as President Bush has rightly said, it is democracy, it is the strength of the ballot, not the bullet, that is more important, and if it's about winning hearts and minds then democracy is very important. I would like the United States to tell General Musharraf please, accept the verdict of the people, hold elections, restore the Constitution.

MITCHELL: Do you think it's so risky at this point that you would not hold rallies or marches? Have you decided one way or another what you want you and your political supporters to do?

BHUTTO: They would like to hold rallies and public demonstrations, but now fundamental human rights have been suspended, and we are going to have to get together to decide what is the best form of protest. But there will be a protest. Whether it's a public meeting, whether it's a sit-in, there will be protests, because it's very difficult to keep quiet in the face of the suspension of the Constitution of Pakistan, which amounts to a military rule. They would like to see the restoration of the Constitution, and I would like to urge General Musharraf to restore the Constitution, to accept the verdict of the court, even if it's a verdict that he does not like. Because we can only strengthen the rule of law if we accept the verdict of the court. And I would like to ask

Washington not to put everything behind one man, but to put it behind the people of Pakistan. People of my country must know that the international community and the world's only superpower stands with them rather than with an individual.

Mohtarma Benazir Bhutto's Address to Diplomats at PPP Foreign Liaison Committee Reception - Senate Hall - Islamabad

Ladies and gentlemen

I appreciate the opportunity to have this conversation with you, especially at this most critical time in the history of my nation.

Obviously Pakistan is at a turning point, and the direction we follow will not only impact the future of my nation, but I strongly believe will have a direct and immediate impact on the stability of the region and the stability of the world.

I take this opportunity to thank the international community for their support to the people of Pakistan in calling upon General Musharaf to lift the curbs of the media, release political prisoners, retire as Army Chief on schedule, and hold elections on schedule.

Democracy is morally right, and even more important to this forum, democracy is the only viable way to contain the growth of extremism, militancy and fanaticism that now threatens the world.

My party, nation and I have spent our lives fighting for democracy and for democratic governance. They are fighting now for democracy to safeguard people's rights and also to safeguard the unity of Pakistan. Their goal is to ensure that through empowerment, employment and education, regions of my country cease being the Petri dish for international and national terrorist plots that threaten us all.

Pakistan under dictatorship is a pressure cooker. Without a place to vent, the passion of our people for liberty threatens to explode. The current military dictatorship that rules my country with an iron fist is opposing the inevitable forces of history. There is not enough barbed wire, or bullets, or bayonets to defeat my people's unquestionable desire for democracy, for control over their own lives, for human rights, gender equality, labour and minority rights and for a chance to build a better life for their children. These are indeed the dreams of the Pakistani people and of all people. These are universal values.

It is eleven years since the destabilization of the democratic government I led but it has failed to crush the will and support of the people for a representative government that addresses the bread and butter issues of our people, 74 per cent of whom live in poverty. Poverty has increased as has joblessness since the PPP government, with a 6 per cent growth rate, without 10 billions of aid, was overthrown.

Yesterday my home was surrounded and I was unofficially put under house arrest because this military regime did not want the world to see that the people of Pakistan want change, want freedom, and want liberty. The garrison town of Pindi was cut off and surrounded. With blockades, barbed wire and the motorway closed. For 8 hours people were gassed and beaten. The brutal images of police beating innocent women were on every television screen on Earth. Tomorrow people of Sindh will hold protest meetings in every district to show solidarity with the people of Rawalpindi.

In Pakistan we say that there are two tests for the success of a public meeting. When the government does not use coercive methods to stop a meeting, the success is judged by the number of people present.

On October 18 the people of Pakistan held the most historic rally in the history of Pakistan when three million turned out in Karachi, stretching all the way back on the National Highway to receive me to express their hope that my return would be a catalyst of a change from dictatorship to democracy.

The second test of a popular public meeting is the amount of police force and measures used to block the peoples participation. The amount of force and restrictive measures is proportionate to the number of people expected to turn out and attend a public meeting.

Force was used to bring closure of Northern Pakistan on November 9, 2007. There was tear-gassing, baton charging, arrest of 5000 activists, including women parliamentarians from Peshwar to Rawalpindi, Karachi to Pindi, Lahore to Pindi and Islamabad to Pindi. The amount of force used was, according to our calculation,to stop a gathering of a million people. By both tests, coercive and non-coercive, the people rose to the occasion.

Now the ball is in the regime's court. They have called for a Long March from Lahore from November 13, 2007. This is the March for Freedom, freedom from dictatorship, from militancy from poverty and unemployment

The current regime has convinced some Nations that General Musharaf alone stands in the way of a nuclear armed, fundamentalist Pakistan. This is a misperception. The religious parties in Pakistan have never received more than 11% of the vote in any election and they would receive less today. It is dictatorship that fuels extremism. The dictatorship of 80's created the Afghan Mujahideen which morphed into Taliban and Al-Qaeda. The political partners of that dictatorship hold key positions in the political, administrative and security institutions of this dictatorship. They cannot, and have not contained extremism nor reduced poverty. They have exacerbated the situation to an extent where nuclear armed Pakistan is threatened with implosion.

Only a popularly elected democratic government with the mandate of the people has the political base to undermine the militants and bring peace to the people of Pakistan.

Dictatorship does not contain fanaticism. Dictatorship causes fanaticism. Ladies and gentlemen, Pakistan plays a central role in the direction of one billion Muslims on this planet. A Pakistan which is moderate, enlightened, modern can be a model to the people in the Muslim world who have to choose between the forces of the past and the forces of the future. Pakistan can be critical to democratic development and the containment of extremism all over Asia and Africa, and can spare our global community further senseless attacks from the forces of hatred.

The enemies of reconciliation amongst our peoples and our nations are trying desperately to provoke a clash of civilizations. These fanatics thrive on chaos. They thrive on the desperation that comes from dictatorship. Democracy suffocates them by giving people choices and giving people hope.

The PPP and I negotiated with General Musharaf's regime for a peaceful transition to democracy. They worked on a road map for fair elections and transition to democracy.

Tragically, suddenly General Musharaf suspended the constitution and imposed Martial Law. This Martial law has been called an Emergency for International consumption.

The PPP has called upon General Musharaf to:

1. Revive the Constitution and with it the judges.
2. Retire as Chief of Army Staff on November 15 as scheduled.
3. Hold general elections called on November 15 on schedule for January 15, 2008.
4. Re-constitute the Election Commission and implement election reforms including an interim government of national consensus to oversee the elections, suspension of the Mayors for the elections period, appointment of impartial officials to important government positions, a fair voter account, no improvised polling stations and other such measures.
5. End of political victimization
6. Lifting of curbs on the media.

Pakistan is in a crisis. Their country, armed forces, police, women, judges, lawyers, minorities, labour, peasants, students, intellectuals and youth are under assault, some by the militants, others by the military regime.

The choice must not be between the military or the militants the choice must be for the will of the people, for democracy. If for no other reason than your own national self-interest, stand with us in our demand for free and fair elections with robust international monitoring.

The Taliban are coming nearer and nearer. I do not want to be melodramatic. But it is the harsh reality that they came from the mountains of Tora Bora to the tribal areas. First one agency fell, then another as the government struck ceasefires and peace treaties with them. Bajaur fell, Khyber fell, Waziristan fell. Now towns in Swat are falling. Madyan fell, Kalam fell. Today they knock on the doors of Shangla Hills.

The Freedom March, the caravan of democracy is not about Benazir Bhutto. This is not a about the Pakistan Peoples Party. This is about saving Pakistan from disintegration at the hands of militants who have grown in strength under a military dictatorship. They threaten us all. The people of Pakistan cannot be allowed to fall from one dictatorship to another, from military dictatorship to religious dictatorship. I have returned to help my people. My supporters, often from working families, often young, are risking their lives to save Pakistan by saving democracy. My Father gave his life for the democratic rights of the people.

They don't accept tyranny. Their cause is just, our path is right for it is the path of truth, the path of the people. They appeal to all the people of our country to walk with us on our common destination towards freedom. They ask the international community to give us moral support.

They believe that victory and defeat are in the hands of God, as is life and death, but we must do what is right, what is just. They must raise our voices and begin the journey in the great walk from tyranny to freedom.

Thank you!

Bibliography

Abbott, Freeland. "Pakistan and the Secular State." Pages 352-70 in Donald E. Smith, ed., *South Asian Politics and Religion*, Princeton: Princeton University Press, 1966.

Abbott, Freeland. *Islam and Pakistan.* Ithaca: Cornell University Press, 1968.

Abdullah Malik, (1988), *Bhutto se Benazir tak: Siyasi tajziye, Maktabah-yi Fikr o Danish*, ASIN B0000CRQJH

Adams, Charles J. "The Ideology of Mawlana Maududi." Pages 371-97 in Donald E. Smith, ed., *South Asian Politics and Religion*, Princeton: Princeton University Press, 1966.

Afzal, M. Rafique. *Political Parties in Pakistan*, 1947-1958. Islamabad: National Commission on Historical and Cultural Research, 1976.

Agnihotri, V.K., " *Indian History*", Allied Publishers Limited, New Delhi.

Bahadur, Lal. *The Muslim League: Its History, Activities and Achievements.* Lahore: Book Traders, 1979.

Basham, A.L. *The Wonder That Was India.* New York: Grove Press, 1954.

Biographical Encyclopaedia of Pakistan, Biographical Research Institute of Pakistan, Lahore.

Callard, Keith. *Pakistan: A Political Study.* London: Allen and Unwin, 1957.

Callard, Keith. *Pakistan's Foreign Policy: An Interpretation.* New York: Institute of Pacific Relations, 1959.

Callard, Keith. *Political Forces in Pakistan: 1947-1959.* New York: Institute of Pacific Relations, 1959.

Case, Margaret H. *South Asia History, 1750-1950: A Guide to Periodicals, Dissertations, and Newspapers.* Princeton: Princeton University Press, 1968.

Chaudhry, G.W., "*Constitutional Development in Pakistan*", Longman, U.K., 1969.

Chaudhry, G.W., "*The Last Days of United Pakistan*", C. Hurst and Company, London, 1974.

Diane Sansevere-Dreher, (1991), *Benazir Bhutto* (Changing Our World Series), Bantam Books (Mm), ISBN 0553158570

Economic Survey 1996-97, Finance Division, Government of Pakistan.

Encyclopaedia of Asian History, Asian Society USA, 1988.

Hall, Carla, "The April of Her Freedom Five Years Later, Benazir Bhutto's Plea for Pakistan", *Washington Post,* April 4, 1984

Hamid, Abdul, "Muslim Separatism in India".

Haque, "Liaquat A. Khan's tour of America", *The Pakistan Times,* October 16, 1986.

Haque, S. M. Izharul, "A dedicated life", *The Pakistan Times,* October 27, 1992.

Ikram, Dr. S. M., "*Modern Muslim India and the Birth of Pakistan*", Institute of Islamic Culture, Lahore, 1990.

Ikram, Dr. S. M., "*Muslim Rule in India and Pakistan*", Students Books Aid, Karachi, 1991.

Iqbal Akhund, (2000), *Trial and Error: The Advent and Eclipse of Benazir Bhutto,* OUP Pakistan, ISBN 0195791606

Iqbal Akhund, (2002), *Benazir Hukoomat: Phela Daur, Kia Khoya, Kia Paya?,* OUP Pakistan, ISBN 0195794214

Kadri, Justice Syed Shameem Hussain, "*Creation of Pakistan*", Wajidalis Ltd., Lahore, 1982.

Katherine M. Doherty, Caraig A. Doherty , (1990), *Benazir Bhutto* (Impact Biographies Series), Franklin Watts.

Kureshy, K. U., "*Geography of Pakistan*", National Book Service, Lahore, 1986.

Libby Hughes, (2000), *Benazir Bhutto: From Prison to Prime Minister*, Backinprint.Com, ISBN 0595003885

Life Sketch of Jatoi, *The Frontier Post*, Peshawar, August 9, 1990.

Lubna Rafique, (1994), *Benazir & British Press*, 1986-1990, Gautam, ASIN B0000CP41S.

M. Fathers, (1992), *Biography of Benazir Bhutto*, W.H. Allen / Virgin Books, ISBN 024554965X.

Mahmud, S. F., "*A Short History of Islam*", Oxford University Press, 1995.

Mary Englar, (2007), *Benazir Bhutto: Pakistani Prime Minister and Activist*, Compass Point Books.

Mazhar-Ul-Haq, "*The 1973 Constitution of Pakistan*", Bookland, Lahore, 1993.

Mehmood, Dr. Safdar, "*Pakistan Political Roots and Development*", Vanguard, Lahore, 1990.

Nasir, M. Saeed; Hyder, Syed Kamal, "*Economics of Pakistan*", Educon Publication, Lahore, 1993-94.

Niazi, Kausar, "*Zulfikar Ali Bhutto of Pakistan: Last Days*", Vikas Publishing House Pvt. Ltd.

Pakistan Basic Facts, Directorate General of Films and Publications, Government of Pakistan.

Pakistan Studies for Intermediate Classes, Sh. Shaukat Ali and Sons, Karachi, 1983.

Pas Manzar: *Ghulam Ishaq Khan*, The Imroze, Lahore, December 16, 1988.

Quaid-i-Azam Muhammad Ali Jinnah Speeches and Statements 1947-48", Ministry of Information and Broadcasting, Directorate of Films and Publications, Elite Publishers Pvt. Ltd. Karachi, 1989.

Qureshi, I. H., "*A Short History of Pakistan*", University of Karachi, 1992.

Qureshi, I. H., "*Struggle for Pakistan*", University of Karachi, 1965.

Rabbani, M. Ikram; Sayyid, Monawwar Ali, "*An Introduction to Pakistan Studies*", The Caravan Book House, Lahore, 1995.

Rafiq Zakaria (1990). *The Trial of Benazir.* Sangam Books. ISBN 0-861-32265-7.

Rafiq Zakaria, (1991), *The Trial of Benazir Bhutto: An Insight into the Status of Women in Islam,* Eureka Pubns, ISBN 9679783200

Reuters News Agency, "Pakistan Rally Halted before March Begins", *Globe and Mail,* August 29, 1983

Saqib, Ahsan Ullah, "*History of Indo-Pakistan since 1526*", Dogar Brothers, Lahore, 1992.

Sayeed, Dr. Khalid Bin, "*Pakistan: The Formative Phase*".

Sayeed, K. B., "*The Political System of Pakistan*", National Book Service, Lahore.

Sayyid Afzal Haidar, (1996), *Bhutto Trial, National Commission on History & Culture,* ASIN B0000CPBFX

Shaw, Isobel, "*Odyssey Illustrated Guide to Pakistan*", The Guide Book Company Ltd., 1996.

Tadgell, Christopher, "*The History of Architecture in India*", Phaidon Press Ltd., London, 1990.

Talukdar, Mohammad H. R., "*Memories of Huseyn Shaheed Suhrawardy*", United Press Ltd., 1987.

W.F.Pepper, (1983), *Benazir Bhutto,* WF Pepper, ISBN 0946781001.

Wolpert, Stanley, "*Zulfikar Ali Bhutto of Pakistan: His Life and Times*", Oxford University Press, New York, 1993.

INDEX